Interview Strategies That Will Get You the Job You Want

Andrea Kay

Interview Strategies That Will Get You the  Job You Want

ANDREA KAY

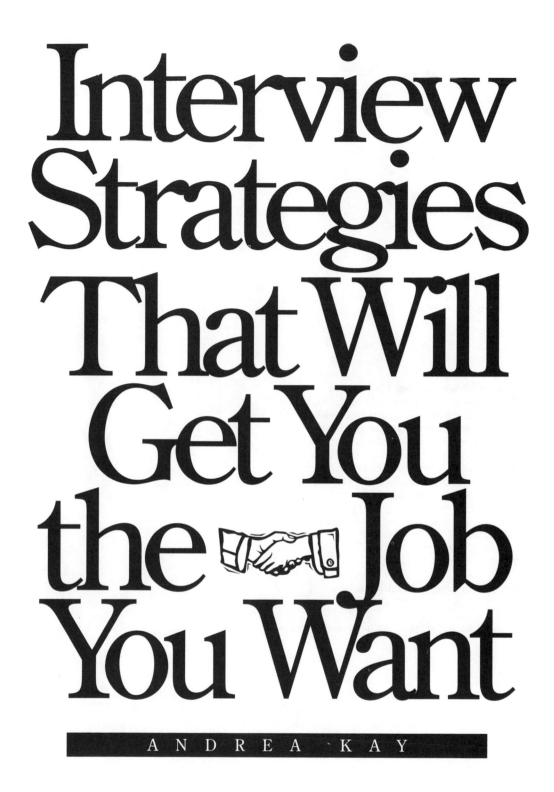

BETTERWAY BOOKS

CINCINNATI, OHIO

Interview Strategies That Will Get You The Job You Want.
Copyright © 1996 by Andrea G. Kay. Printed and bound in the United
States of America. All rights reserved. No part of this book may be
reproduced in any form or by any electronic or mechanical means
including information storage and retrieval systems without
permission in writing from the publisher, except by a reviewer, who
may quote brief passages in a review. Published by Betterway
Books, an imprint of F&W Publications, Inc., 1507 Dana Avenue,
Cincinnati, Ohio 45207. (800) 289-0963. First edition.

Other fine Betterway Books are available from your local bookstore
or direct from the publisher.

00 99 98 97 96   5 4 3 2 1

Library of Congress Cataloging-in-Publication Data

Kay, Andrea G.
    Interview strategies that will get you the job you want / Andrea
G. Kay.
        p.   cm.
    ISBN 1-55870-411-6 (alk. paper)
    1. Employment interviewing.
HF5549.5.I6K38   1996
650.14—dc20   95-49773
                                                         CIP

Edited by Joyce Dolan
Interior design by Brian Roeth

Betterway Books are available at special discounts for sales promotions, premiums and fund-raising use. Special editions or book ex-
cerpts can also be created to specification. For details contact: Special Sales Manager, Betterway Books, 1507 Dana Avenue,
Cincinnati, Ohio 45207.

Information obtained from pages 4 and 73 of *Corporate Quality Universities* by Jeanne C. Meister is © 1994, and is reprinted by permission of Irwin Professional Publishing.

Dedication

To my dad, for my incessant-curiosity genes and ana-lytical side of the brain. To my mother, for my persis-tence and sensitivity to what I say and how I say it. And to whomever threw in the creative spirit that frees me to be whatever I choose.

To Greg and his divine stories.

ABOUT THE AUTHOR

Andrea Kay is a career consultant, has written over four hundred articles on careers and job hunting as writer of the weekly newspaper column "Ask Andrea" since 1988, and is host of the radio talk show, "Job Talk," which she started in 1991. She also gives weekly career advice on a CBS-Television affiliate.

She has counseled hundreds of job hunters and presented dozens of seminars on interviewing skills and strategies to people in all types of professions from Fortune 500 companies to small and nonprofit businesses.

Her will to create the job of her dreams, along with her background in communications and as an advertising copywriter, honed the skills necessary to help people package and position themselves in the marketplace.

She's been widely quoted and interviewed in publications that include *U.S. Air Magazine*, *Redbook*, *Woman* and other U.S. business newspapers. She also wrote and narrated the videotape *Common Mistakes in Interviews and How to Overcome Them*, published by Cambridge Educational.

Recognition for her contributions includes the Women In Communications Gem Award for adherence to the highest standards of practice in professional communications, support of women in the workforce and being a friend to job seekers.

She is a sought-after keynote and workshop presenter, speaking to national professional groups who named her Outstanding Speaker and Program of the Year. She has also been invited to address state and federal legislators on the plight of white-collar workers.

Andrea received her B.A. degree from Kent State University, and her continuing education includes course work in Gestalt stress management, building self-esteem, use of self in psychotherapy, Spanish, painting and drawing. She lives in Cincinnati, Ohio.

ACKNOWLEDGMENTS

THANKS

Each person who helped me with this book is either a specialist in his or her field or just plain smart. Some of them I've never met. And in a faster-than-speed-of-light world, it just goes to show that people will take time from their harried lives, deadlines and crises to help. The least I can do is say thank you:

To Larry Leith at the U.S. Bureau of Labor Statistics. Your tax money is well spent with him in Washington. He is thorough and witty, and was willing to thumb though pages of boring data to help me come up with the statement I make in chapter one.

To these professionals, who really know their stuff:

Recruiters Howard Rogers and Bill Radin; Sherry Kinsella, who knows about search committees; Carolyn Stendahl and Cleve Campbell of Belcan Temporaries, who know the temporary business inside and out; Angela McDermott, who has big-company insight, understands how organizations and people work together and overall, has good judgment; Joy Dill, who's real smart when it comes to things in general and handling situations with delicacy in particular; Dr. Drema Howard at the University of Kentucky Career Center and Mary Bridget Reilly at the University of Cincinnati.

Authors Joyce Lain Kennedy and Pam Dixon, who somehow understand all this technology about computers. Harvard Law Professor and author John Kotter, who has wisely observed and captured what it takes to succeed in today's workplace.

Attorneys Stephen E. Gillen and William W. Ford III, who can put things so you understand them and generously gave me their time and expertise.

Al Krause, who I've been trying to find a way to thank since 1988, when he let me use his office in San Francisco while I tried to figure out what to do with my life.

My clients, who gave me good and bad examples to share so I could show job hunters what to do and not do.

My friends and family, who didn't see or talk to me for months.

My editor, Joyce Dolan, who was truly a partner.

And finally, my husband, who went beyond the call of marital vows to complete this project with me.

TABLE OF CONTENTS

W. Somerset Maugham said, "It is a funny thing about life:
If you refuse to accept anything but the best, you very often get it."

Strategy Above All Strategies: Read Book Introductions

I have never met anyone who purposely took a job he or she would hate. And yet, I meet hundreds of people who hate their jobs.

You might be one of them. Perhaps you sit behind a computer, a desk, a counter or telephone. You may work in an office building or roam a manufacturing plant. To get your job, you probably put on your most persuasive interview face and may have even said to the employer: "I want this job."

Did the job change once you came on board? Perhaps. Did your boss turn from Jekyll into Hyde? It happens.

I think most people hate their jobs because the job doesn't match up with who they are. It simply doesn't fit. A job that doesn't fit is like wearing clothes that are five sizes too big for you. Or eating vegetarian food every night for dinner when you hate vegetables. You're an adult who can make choices about what you like and dislike, so you're not going to do that, right?

Yet when it comes to careers, people take ill-fitting jobs all the time. It happens because they never defined The Job I Want. No one told them to think about it.

They did, however, get advice such as:

"Get a job that pays well with good benefits."

"Go into health care, there are lots of opportunities."

"Work for the government—you've got a job for life."

"Go with a big company, there's more security."

"Work for Procter & Gamble—it'll look good on your resumé."

"Be a lawyer like your father. There's a job waiting for you."

"Just be glad you have a job in today's economy."

So they took jobs that fit the criteria of well-meaning friends, relatives and teachers. And they were miserable. It's a crummy way to live your life. But many people do—and they come to my office to talk about it. Unfortunately, the tissue box in my office gets a lot of use.

I also see people who have taken ill-fitting jobs because anything looked better than the unhappy situation they were in. Many times, they had been searching for months—even years. They were enticed because someone finally wanted them.

Once a woman called to ask me how to go about switching from being a nurse to being a paralegal.

"Why do you want to do that?" I asked.

"It wouldn't take long to get my certificate," she replied. She didn't have a clue as to whether she'd *like* being a paralegal. It was simply the quickest route to get another decent-paying job.

Is that a good reason to change jobs, not to mention careers? Not in my book (pun intended). Even after I suggested she research this further, she felt it was the best way to go, since it was better than being a nurse. Taking a job because it is the lesser of two evils is not a good reason to change either.

Most of these people believed they *needed* a job. So, like many job hunters, they approached employers with their heads bowed and their hand out.

This thinking—although you're probably not consciously aware of it—programs you to take the job you can get, rather than get the job you want. It puts you in a position of weakness.

You know you're in this position when you're:

- Sitting on the other side of the desk, desperately hoping the interviewer will like you and want to hire you
- Feeling you must sell the interviewer

You don't have to give away your power to get

the job you want. But before you can apply a single interview strategy, you have to define The Job You Want.

No matter what your profession, this is a job that:

- Uses your unique talents and skills
- Fits your personality, style and personal characteristics
- Challenges you to think and grow
- Pays you what you're worth
- Is in an environment that suits your personality, style and values
- Is supported by a management whose values are in alignment with yours
- Is in a business you believe in and support
- Is at a company that appreciates and recognizes your contributions
- Builds on and enhances your expertise and reputation in your field

These are the nine keys to find The Job You Want. You'll have a chance to define The Job You Want in chapter one. Then you will be on your way to creating a picture of what will make you happy. You have a right to it. When you believe that, you will be in a position of strength in the interview. You will make it your responsibility to be an equal partner in this process. The interview will now be an opportunity for:

- You to get information to decide if you want to work for the company (to see if the job fits).
- The employer to get information to decide if he or she wants to hire you (to see if you fit).

This new "positioning" helps you overcome the reason for most interview stress: the intense desire to say and do all the "right" things so you'll get the job. Instead of looking at the interview as a performance in which you must deliver your lines with perfection and persuade your audience to buy you, your goal is to present yourself in the best possible light while you explore if the job is a good fit.

That's just the beginning. You'll need to adopt strategic interview habits to get The Job You Want. You'll learn those in chapters one to ten.

It's not that you aren't qualified; perhaps you are even one of the most talented people in your field. But, folks, here's the way it works: The most qualified people are not necessarily the ones who get

the jobs. It's the people who know how to market themselves who get the jobs. And that small fact of life is nothing to get down and out about. Hey, you've been busy becoming an expert in your field or studying to become one—not an expert interviewer.

You *can* become a savvy interviewer; strategic; someone who understands the interviewer better than the interviewer may understand herself. These chapters are packed with tested techniques and tips on how to do it. Whether you're a novice just out of school or a seasoned professional, you'll learn how to turn the interview from an interrogation into an opportunity. You'll learn what interviewers look for, how they draw information out of you and how they come to conclusions. You'll hear how other people have overcome the same concerns you have.

Your new strategic interview habits will mean knowing:

1. The job you want
2. The interviewer's point of view, goals and fears
3. How to avoid being screened out before the interview
4. What to know before an interview
5. What to expect during the interview
6. What to say and not say
7. When to say what and how to stay in control
8. Why interviewers ask certain questions and how to respond
9. How to handle inappropriate interview questions
10. How to ask for what you want—and get it

Employers will treat you differently as a result. You'll be on equal turf. You might even be the one saying, "Thanks, but no thanks."

That's what you'll learn from this book.

Are you thinking, "But I *do* need a job. I have to pay the bills"?

I know that. Most people work to support themselves and their families. But that doesn't need to be the *sole* reason you work. Especially if you're just beginning your career—now is the time to look for what you want, not just what you can get.

It will be harder to make changes as you get older. You'll have more excuses, more bills and more commitments.

In 1987, I sat down with my calculator and figured

out that if I worked fifty weeks a year for forty years, I'd end up spending eighty thousand hours of my life at my job. That's a lot of time—potentially miserable time.

So I said adios to a public relations and advertising career I'd been in for eleven years, cashed in my frequent flyer miles and hopped a plane to San Francisco to start my six-month sabbatical to figure out if there was a way to make money *and* be fulfilled.

At the time, I was only sure of one thing: I had to do something more meaningful to me than come up with clever ways to promote amusement parks and the sale price of salmon that week. I had to explore this nagging feeling that I was supposed to do more with my life.

I interviewed people about their careers, in the hope of finding out what I could do with mine.

What I learned was that no one else felt fulfilled in their career either. Many said they weren't using their skills or education. Some had been laid off from their jobs and didn't know how to look for a job they'd like, or even what that job would be. They didn't like their bosses. They couldn't get along with co-workers. They counted the seconds until five o'clock or the weekend when they could do what they really wanted.

Except for an old high school acquaintance, friends of my parents, someone's sister, the owner of the Chinese restaurant where I got take-out every night and the cashier at the grocery store where I bought cappuccino every morning, I didn't know too many people. So I read a lot: books with philosophical and spiritual themes, business texts on management, leadership and re-engineering, and magazines about trends and the future. I wrote down lists of things I loved to do and dreams about what I wanted to be. It included being a newspaper columnist, giving seminars and somehow doing work that was important to the world.

My brain was full. But my soul was empty. I remember the evening I was driving back to the East Bay where I was staying, passing all these people who had normal lives. There was an apartment complex where couples were grilling out on their patios. I passed a strip mall where people were walking out of restaurants, arm in arm, laughing.

As much as I knew I was heading down a neces-

sary path . . . that this was part of the process . . . I couldn't stand the uncertainty. I decided to take the rest of my savings and buy a full-size advertisement in *The Wall Street Journal*. I would pour out my heart in this ad, and hopefully someone would read it and call me up and offer me the job that included my skills *and* my dreams. Then I flew back to Cincinnati to wait for the phone call.

It's funny how something always happens when things seem to be at their darkest. I did get a phone call—luckily before I blew my entire savings. I heard from a friend in San Diego. "What am I going to do with my life?" I moaned to my friend.

"You're really good at listening to people and helping them get to the core problem of something," he said. "You're interested in business and you like helping people. I know someone who does career consulting. Why don't you look into that?"

"What's that?" I asked.

"I'm not sure, I just know he helps people figure out their careers."

I looked up "Careers" in the yellow pages. I called the companies listed and asked them if they had any literature. I read everything I could find on it. I wrote the best letter I could to one of the company presidents. He called and we met for an "informational interview." He explained what career counseling was all about. The more he explained the process—which included giving seminars—the more I realized it fit my skills, natural talents and interests. It was a field I had never encountered but one I knew I wanted to explore. It just felt absolutely right.

At the end of our second meeting a week later, I made him an offer. I told him I could help promote his company with my skills and background if he would train me in his business.

The story goes real fast from this point on. He offered me a job and I accepted.

Some days it was a very sad job. Listening to people's stories about how they were fired because the company eliminated their department . . . about finding out their jobs were no longer needed because of new technology or no more funding . . . about getting fired for the second time in a year and not understanding why—and no one was willing to tell them.

On top of that, they had to go "out there" and

compete with hundreds of other competent, qualified and bright people. Employers didn't return phone calls. Knowing someone who knew someone in a company didn't guarantee them a job. A perfect attendance record, glowing performance appraisals or a college degree didn't get them a job.

Job hunting was similar to what singer Martha Reeves said it was like to make it in the music industry: "You were in the recording studio and if you couldn't get the song in two takes there was always someone waiting in the wings."

Other days the job was incredibly inspiring—when people were willing to do what it took to meet their goals and dreams.

So that brings me back to my point about going after what you want, as opposed to what you can get. It's tempting to do the latter.

But do you want to ramble through your career, job to job . . . wondering, is this all there is? . . . complaining about a jerky boss or a job you hate to get up for . . . worrying whether you'll have a job next week?

How do you want to spend those eighty thousand hours of your life? It will be up to you.

In fact, it's a requirement. More and more companies expect you to be self-reliant. Their policies reflect the new theme of employee self-management that asks you to identify career goals and take more responsibility for financial security and health care expenses.

They encourage it . . . they nudge workers to contribute more to retirement plans . . . bring in financial planning experts to meet employees over lunch . . . replace traditional pension plans with ones in which contributions are based on profit.

There is no such thing as job security, so you might as well give it up. There's also no such thing as the perfect job. But you can start on a journey that helps you understand where you *do* want to go, which will be the closest thing you can get to security.

In the end, it will be worth it. Because it's incredibly liberating and fulfilling to be headed down a path that feels right for you.

At the 1993 Academy Awards ceremony, Clint Eastwood and Al Pacino both said, accepting their awards, that they were lucky to be able to make their life's work something they enjoy. That "luck" did not just happen. People create their own luck with a combination of optimism and hope about their future, a sense of realism, the willingness to ask themselves penetrating questions, give honest answers and take action to meet their goals.

This book will help you do that when it comes to getting The Job You Want.

For now, you may have to accept or stay in a job just to pay the bills. These are temporary situations to help you take care of your needs. Take care of these immediate goals first. You won't have everything the way you want it. It will come in stages. Comedian Stephen Wright said, "You can't have everything. Where would you put it?"

This book and the strategies I cover are for people who believe they have the right to enjoy the majority of their time—the time they spend in their work.

Let me put it another way. Pretend you just won the lottery. Eighteen million big ones. You won't have to work another day in your life. But if you enjoy making a contribution to society, have talents and skills and want to be valued and rewarded for them, you will still seek ways to do that. The difference is, now you feel free to look for the job you want, instead of the job you need.

As you learn these interview strategies, remember that feeling of freedom you just had when you didn't need a job. The odds of winning an $18 million lottery are slim. Your odds are better that, with the right interview strategies, you'll get the job you want.

I'm a Believer

Strategy #1

**Believe you have a right to be happy
in your work and get the job you want.**

The Job You Want doesn't necessarily have a title such as lawyer, nurse, social worker, publicist, truck driver or bookkeeper. In fact, at this point it's best *not* to give it a job title.

What??? No job title? How will people know who I am? How will *I* know who I am? That's good, get it out of your system now. Because if we're going to make any headway, we have to prepare you to change the way you see yourself and your work. From now on, you'll define the job you want in terms of exactly that: *what you want.*

Remember the nine key elements I listed in the Introduction that define The Job You Want, no matter what your profession? You're going to care about some of these elements more than others. After working with hundreds of people in all types of professions, I am utterly convinced that these are what make for happy, fulfilled workers—to one degree or another.

THE JOB YOU WANT HAS THE FOLLOWING NINE KEY ELEMENTS:
- Uses your unique talents and skills
- Fits your personality, style and personal characteristics
- Challenges you to think and grow
- Pays you what you're worth
- Is in an environment that suits your personality, style and values
- Is supported by a management whose values are in alignment with yours
- Is in a business you believe in and support

- Operates within a structure that appreciates and recognizes your contributions
- Builds on and enhances your expertise and reputation in your field

Before you can get this job, you have to define it. So let's do that. Get some paper. You're going to do nine exercises that will help you create a picture of the job you want.

THE MUSIC THAT MAKES YOU DANCE
Your Unique Talents and Skills

These are the skills you use when you're so engrossed in what you're doing, you forget to eat. (OK, you would have forgotten if your stomach wasn't growling so loudly.)

They are your *strengths*—the skills you enjoy using most and that come most naturally to you. If you don't know what yours are, here's a way to determine them.

- First, write down ten things in your life that you consider achievements.

These are things you've been involved in that you enjoyed, are proud of and can describe a result. Don't limit this list to work-related achievements. Think about things you've done in your community, school or organizations you belong to, and events you've participated in, as well as projects on the job.

Don't say you don't have any. I simply don't buy that.

An achievement does not have to be something that others think is exceptional or fantastic. We're not talking Guiness Book of World Records or No- bel Prizes here. If you're proud of it and enjoyed doing it, that's all that matters.

Examples:

- As manager of a retail operation, I was instru- mental in opening two new stores and within a two-year period, increasing the customer base by 50 percent.
- As a marketing professional, I led a team that acquired a key account and increased mar- ket share by 35 percent.
- As a human resource professional, I handled a sensitive personnel situation that turned a marginally performing employee into a sig- nificant contributor.
- As a volunteer, I organized a team, gained commitments from individuals and busi- nesses, and coordinated activities for build- ing a new home for a needy family.
- After a major earthquake, I led and coordi- nated volunteers to help restore electricity and communications, distribute food and medical supplies, direct rescue efforts and transport and evacuate people.
- I created quality teams and mandated train- ing, turning around a department that was losing money and had the highest turnover in the company.
- I developed promotional campaigns for our group's fundraising events, annual senior picnic and awards dinner that increased membership by 30 percent.

• Next, analyze each achievement. Ask your- self—and write down—the skills and abilities it took to accomplish that achievement.

To illustrate how to do this, let's analyze two of the examples I just listed.

If you were the manager who was instrumental in the opening of two new stores, what did it take to do that? The ability to:

analyze	coordinate
research	persuade
follow through on	prioritize
details	problem solve
envision	work well with people
organize	develop procedures

plan	be a team player
train	write
monitor	communicate
motivate	present
create	manage
promote	work with computers
lead	

You probably never realized you were doing all that, did you? You thought you were just opening two new stores.

If you were the human resource professional who handled a sensitive personnel situation, what did that take? It took these skills:

train	organize
analyze	mediate
negotiate	persuade
communicate	follow through
write	work well with people
monitor	

. . . the list goes on.

• Now analyze *your* ten achievements. You were hoping I wasn't going to say that, weren't you? "Can't I just take a test?" you're saying. "Isn't this information in some other book? What about a Ouija board?" Nope, nada, no way, José. You can't skip this.

Magical things will happen when you do this ex- ercise. You'll find that many of the same skills pop up again and again. You'll also see patterns in what you enjoy doing most. And later on, you'll use this information for another interview strategy.

• After you've completed analyzing all ten, de- velop a master list of all your skills. That's easy.

• Then prioritize these skills according to what you enjoy doing most. That's harder. Just keep ask- ing yourself, which of these do I like to do most? Second most, etc.

What are the first six to eight words on your list? Write each one on a card or separate piece of paper.

Now define these six to eight words further. If you've got the words "problem solve" on a card, let your imagination go. What kinds of problems do you love to solve? Operational? Administrative? Re- lationship problems?

If you've got the word "coordinate" on a card,

what do you want to coordinate? Meetings, information, conferences, parties? If you enjoy research, what do you want to research? If you like to write, what do you write? And so on.

These six to eight phrases will be your strongest skills—or strengths. Most people can't just rattle these off because, as you can see, it takes thought, analysis and prioritization.

Example:

After analyzing his achievements and prioritizing his skills according to what he enjoys most, here are the retail manager's strengths:

- Coordinate and present training
- Lead and motivate employees
- Solve operational problems
- Create strategic sales promotions
- Analyze financial data
- Envision and plan complex projects

The student who developed promotional campaigns for her group's fund-raising events, annual senior picnic and awards dinner and increased membership by 30 percent analyzed these and other achievements and then prioritized her skills in terms of what she enjoys doing the most. Her strengths came up as:

- Create and write promotional copy
- Visualize and develop graphics and layout
- Analyze product benefits and persuade potential buyers
- Inspire and lead others to meet goals
- Coordinate details related to printing and graphic production

After you do this exercise, on a separate piece of paper write this heading: *"My unique talents and skills."* Then list your strengths.

Your Personality, Style and Personal Characteristics

There's no right or wrong way to be—you are who you are. You like to do something one way; someone else has a completely different style and way of doing it. Your style of doing things depends on your personal characteristics.

To help you identify your characteristics, go back to your achievements and write down words that

describe *how* you did them. Here are some examples:

persistent	self-motivated
politically astute	resourceful
trustworthy	cautious
accurate	adaptable
calm	practical
orderly	sensitive
firm	economical
diplomatic	good in crisis
flexible	supportive
cooperative	perceptive
innovative	take-charge
dynamic	assertive
tactful	precise
mature	articulate
responsible	disciplined
caring	committed
ambitious	detail-oriented
energetic	creative
persevering	profit-oriented
fast-learner	empathetic
independent	realistic
fair	courteous
project-oriented	consistent
thorough	patient

Write out the heading: *"My personal characteristics"* and list the results of your analysis.

What Challenges You

Everyone is challenged and stimulated by different things:

- Learning new ideas and techniques
- Analyzing problems
- Researching facts
- Persuading someone to buy something
- Changing an opinion
- Exceeding limits
- Experimenting
- Designing something new
- Discovering something new
- Exploring a new place

What challenges you to think and grow? Again, go back to your achievements and things you've enjoyed in your life. What did you find challenging?

Write out this heading: *"What challenges me"* and list your results.

Your Worth

Your worth—or what you are paid—depends on how much experience and responsibility you have for the type of position you want. At this point, you may not know what that position or worth is.

But assuming you do know the general area of where you fit in and what such a position might be called, or that you will define it more specifically in the future, you need to know your worth. If you don't know what the salary range is for the position you want, you can research this information. (Chapter four tells you how.)

It's OK to leave this blank for now. When you know this information, write this heading: *"My worth, based on my experience and industry"* and complete it.

Environment That Suits Your Personality, Style, Interests and Values

This may include the culture, hours you work, office politics, whether it's a manufacturing or service industry, in an office, in a plant, outside or a combination of these, working conditions, and whether it's a large or small company. (Small companies allow you to be closer to the decision making, to get involved in many aspects of a business and to have more of an impact. That's also where most of the jobs are.)

For some people, environment means the actual physical surroundings—which may say a lot about the culture. For example, I knew one man who, after college, interviewed at a very large, successful and well-known aerospace manufacturer. His father had worked there his entire career and helped his son get the interview. The young man went through the stringent interview process, took personality and drug tests and was asked to start work on Monday. Monday came and he entered the maximum security gates and drove into a huge parking lot that was surrounded by an eight-foot-tall chain link fence topped with barbed wire and filled with thousands of cars. He parked his car, turned off the ignition— and immediately broke out in a cold sweat. He thought of all the sacrifices his father had made to work at this company for over thirty years. He stared at the fence and felt that if he got out of his car, he would be trapped in the same place for the rest of his life. He started the car and drove home. When he got there, he called personnel and said, "I just can't do it."

This person was very much a free spirit; the environment he would feel comfortable in would be quite different from this. He was lucky to realize it before he started down a path that would confine his spirit.

Another person told me that before an interview she drove to the company and saw an old, decaying building. This woman, always well-dressed and very fashionable, said, "The company just didn't have the image of where I saw myself working."

When you go to interviews you'll want to pay attention to the surroundings and how they feel to you. One woman I know had an interview at a company that was run primarily by engineers. "The place felt like the military. There were beige, yellowed dividers and old furnishings. I wondered, 'Do I want to spend time here?' "

Here is a list to get you thinking about what environment might mean to you:

a lot of structure	competitive
little structure	focuses on quality
work alone	innovative
honest, ethical	loose, laid back
sit at desk all day	focuses on international
leadership with vision	customers
a lot of autonomy	everyone wears a suit
sit at desk half a day	supports continuing
supportive	education
strict hours	wear jeans if you want
office with a window	listens to employee ideas
progressive	contemporary office
flexible hours	work outside
encourages	encourages risk-taking
entrepreneurship	travel 50 percent of the
creative	time
encourages teamwork	service oriented
professional	

Write out this heading: *"Environment I feel comfortable in"* and list the elements important to you.

Your Values

If there's one thing people tend to gripe most about when it comes to their jobs, it's issues about the company's values. Values are principles or standards you consider worthwhile and that are the basis of your decisions and choices. When these conflict, you may be less dedicated, even resentful about going to your job.

I know a freelance graphic designer who is absolutely, positively opposed to the use of tobacco and alcohol in any form. When he was offered a project with a liquor manufacturer, he turned it down. He felt he would compromise his values if he worked on the project.

Other values people consider important in the company they work for fit into the "socially responsible" category, which includes such issues as:

- Family-friendly and gay-friendly policies, including flexible work schedules and child and elder care programs
- Good records on equal employment, women and minority advancement
- Recycling programs
- Not conducting experiments on animals
- Involvement in philanthropic programs
- Using recycled materials to manufacture products

If this sounds like you, you are part of a growing trend in job seekers. These people tend to be less concerned with security and care more about personal enrichment, balance and contributing to society in a more intrinsic way. As a result, they're hunting for companies who also care about more than just the bottom line. Write out the heading: *"Values that are important to me"* and list them.

Businesses You Believe in and Support

Many people tell me they would like to go into sales, but they'd have to believe in whatever it is they are selling. You don't have to be in sales to feel this way. It's much more motivating to go to work every day and do the best you can when you believe in and support the business you're in—no matter what your job. This might go hand in hand with your values.

Other people feel strongly about contributing to a cause or mission.

What businesses would you feel good supporting?

Write out the heading: *"Businesses I could believe in and support"* and list them.

Appreciating and Recognizing Your Contribution

One of the most important needs of people is to be recognized and appreciated for their work and how it contributes to the common goals of the organization. It inspires them to keep doing their best.

Appreciation can be demonstrated through:

Awards	More responsibilities
Promotions	Celebrations
Salary	Public praise
Gifts	Thank-you notes
A pat on the back	

Write out the heading: *"What makes me feel appreciated by management"* and list those things you consider important.

Your Expertise

After working on a certain task or in a particular field, or completing an education, you develop a body of knowledge. Writing it out forces you to think about the depth of what you know, as well as capabilities and expertise you might take for granted.

Here are examples:

IF YOU'VE WORKED IN OR HAVE EXPERTISE IN:	YOU MIGHT KNOW ABOUT:
Financial services	financial planning, retirement and estate planning, investments, regulatory compliance, portfolio management, securities
Project management	writing proposals and contracts, contract administration, team building, leadership, management, computers, training, accounts payable, purchase orders, estimating, inventory control, vendor relations
Sales or marketing	trade shows, media relations, fund raising, strategic planning, sales, training, annual reports, market research, territory management, sales forecasting

IF YOU'VE WORKED IN OR HAVE EXPERTISE IN:	YOU MIGHT KNOW ABOUT:
Administrative support	word processing, managing executives' calendars, customer service, travel arrangements, handling sensitive documents, ordering supplies
Managing your home and family and volunteer work	nutrition, meal planning, special event planning, overseeing projects, coordinating details, organizing and planning, teaching, motivating, budgeting, promoting
Engineering	estimating, scheduling, equipment design, technology, robotics, inventory control
Maintenance	machine repairs, asbestos control, hazardous chemicals, blueprint reading, OSHA, NIOSH and EPA regulations
Graphic design	graphics, logos, desktop publishing, printing processes, newsletters and brochures
Marketing analysis	forecasting, statistical analysis, systems development, cluster analysis, market segmentation, product testing
Law	patent applications and legislation, licensing agreements, acquisitions, joint ventures, intellectual property, trademarks, copyrights, environmental law, business litigation
Landscaping	horticulture, plants, gardening, supervision, chemical pest control, power tools, turf management, pruning techniques, botanical sites
Hospitality	catering, customer service, special event planning, convention services, decor, logistics, scheduling, budgets, theme parties, housekeeping, room service
Construction	crew supervision, welding, schematic diagrams and blueprints, power tools, heavy equipment operation, HVAC

Even if you just received your degree, you have stockpiled knowledge of many things. You've had exposure to teams (if you worked in groups or on committees) and leadership (if you were involved in projects and groups).

One of my clients had recently completed her education in Health Services Administration and an internship at a retirement home. After thinking about her classes and hands-on experience, here's some of what we came up with:

- Exposure to total quality management, strategic management, accounting, finance, budgeting and teams
- Solid understanding of adult development, psychological aging and ethics related to the elderly
- Familiar with community-based services
- Proficient in computers
- Operations and customer service

Write out the heading: *"My expertise—or area(s) in which I want to become an expert"* and list the knowledge you have accumulated.

TRANSLATION, PLEASE

I'm assuming you just spent hours accumulating all these pages of headings and notes. Now you're wondering, "What does it tell me? Now can I look for the job I want?" Patience.

This work doesn't necessarily translate into a specific job title or even a particular industry. Jobs—especially these days and into the future—do not fit into neat little boxes.

STOP THE WORLD, I WANNA GET ON

Jobs—their titles and their functions—keep changing because the world keeps changing. For example, someone who called herself a nurse in the past probably worked in hospitals for much of her career. Today, hospitals are cutting costs: reducing the number of nurses and handing their duties to aides and assistants.

Now nurses are finding jobs in home health care

operations, private medical practices or as consultants to places like insurance companies and health maintenance organizations. If someone with an R.N. degree who has always worked in a hospital markets herself simply based on her past title and the environment in which she had jobs, she severely limits her opportunities. But if she describes herself in terms of the elements we just went through, she opens up a world of options. In addition, she is more likely to get the job she wants.

Let me show you. If we apply the nine key elements, she might describe herself as:

1. Having *strengths* to administer medications and give primary care, supervise other licensed and unlicensed nursing staff, monitor quality of care, research and write policies and procedures and present training
2. Having *personal characteristics* such as empathy, self-discipline, maturity, enthusiasm and independence
3. *Challenged by* assessing, designing and teaching new ideas and concepts to people
4. *Having a worth* of $40,000 to $47,000 a year
5. *Comfortable in an environment* where there is a lot of autonomy, flexible hours, supportive management and leadership with a vision
6. *Having values* that support the advancement of minorities and women
7. *Supportive of a company that* delivers quality health care
8. *Wanting to be appreciated through* promotions and public praise
9. Having *expertise* in clinical instruction, nurse recruitment, hiring and performance evaluations, working with social service agencies and nursing homes, hospital policies and procedures, insurance, medical libraries, needs of the elderly and nutrition

Knowing what she wants helps her research:

- What kinds of organizations need people who can do what she does and utilize her knowledge and expertise
- What organizations might call that role in today's changing work environment
- Which organizations can offer her a position or even how she can create a position for herself

This position may or may not be in a hospital. It might be a permanent job in a university setting, a training company or an insurance company. Or it could describe a consultant.

I'll use myself as another example. When I told people what I was pursuing in my next career, I never would have done it successfully if I had said:

"Hi, I've been in public relations and an advertising copywriter for the past eleven years and now I want to be a career consultant."

Huh? People just wouldn't get the connection. Instead, I told people about my:

- *Strengths* as a communicator, writer and entrepreneur, in building interpersonal relationships, asking questions and creative problem solving, and my intense curiosity about people and information
- *Desire* to help others
- *Strong interest* in business, self improvement and human behavior
- *Experience* in helping companies package, position and market their products and services

This, they saw, could translate into someone who listened to people and their concerns, helped them write marketing tools, and position and package them to market themselves. They could see that as I developed my expertise I would be knowledgeable enough to write articles and give speeches on this subject. I led them to this understanding by the information I shared and the way I presented it.

I marketed myself as a body of skills and talents that could help solve a problem.

This approach also makes you incredibly equipped to find and create jobs.

Let me explain. At least ten people a month say to me:

1. I need help finding what's available.
2. I need help figuring out where the jobs are.
3. I need help in knowing what's out there.

This is completely backward thinking.

People seem to think there are all these openings "out there" and if only somebody like me would share that secret knowledge on how to find them, *voila!*

Now if you're like most people, when I say that, you're thinking, "Well, I know no one can do that."

But isn't that what you think you *need*? Come on now, 'fess up, don't you believe, somewhere deep inside, that it sure would make things a whole lot easier if you just knew what's available?

But believe me, it's not going to happen. It doesn't exist.

What *does* exist is a world full of problems. People in companies who need people who can make their computers work better and faster, their sales double and triple, their customers happier, their operations smoother, their communications stronger, their employees more knowledgeable and their markets bigger.

If you know what kinds of problems you solve and skills you have and present that information to the right people in a logical, passionate format, you will discover where that job fits into the world.

Knowing this will steer you away from the misguided thinking of filling openings and instead guide you to go after the job you want. When someone asks you what you want to do, you will no longer be tempted to say, "It depends on what's out there . . . what's available."

Well then, you're thinking, "How do I know what the problems are and who's got them?"

Start with your daily newspaper. Read business magazines. Look at your own life: What problems do you face? What processes need improvement?

The business section in your newspaper will tell you who might be addressing these problems . . . which companies are expanding or diversifying . . . moving or growing. Read who applied for building permits and acquired land. Many newspapers have a page in their business section that lists government contracts awarded, commercial property transfers, commercial construction projects or renovations and new accounts awarded to advertising agencies.

Here's an example. A tiny article appeared in the newspaper in 1995, saying Ameritech, the Midwest BabyBell, is getting into the security business by creating a new subsidiary to design, install and maintain security systems. This is to make it more convenient for customers to remotely monitor and adjust their heating, air conditioning and lighting.

What will Ameritech's problems and needs be? They'll not only need people to design, install and maintain these security systems, but to market

them. The jobs may not exist yet, but they will.

The other piece of information an article like this tells you is that there is a need out there to meet customers' demands for more convenient ways to monitor and secure their property. How can you turn that into a job? What kinds of skills will be needed?

Here's another example. In 1995, grave concerns were raised over the deaths and injuries due to hospital-based mistakes—many of them due to medication errors. Studies showed that these errors were the fault of bad organization, not bad doctors. These mistakes are preventable. It was the systems' failures that led to the mistakes. These systems include:

- Doctors' lack of knowledge about a drug, the right times to use it, its correct dose or forms it comes in.
- Mistaken identity of drugs with names that look or sound alike
- Doctors not having enough information about the patient (such as what other medications they're taking)
- Pharmacists not getting lab results to ensure the prescription was right

What are some solutions?

- A better way to identify look-alike or sound-alike drugs
- A quick and easy way for doctors to get information about a drug

. . . and so on.

Depending on your skills, interests, background and expertise, is there a way to create a job for yourself here?

Also, look for trends. *The Futurist* magazine listed some of the rising trends of the 1990s as:

- Environmental cleanup
- Waste disposal
- Health care services
- Biotechnology
- Retirement communities and nursing homes
- Home entertainment
- Space commercialization
- Infrastructure rehabilitation
- Health and convenience foods

- Space-age materials
- Time-saving devices
- Highway and air-traffic congestion
- Recordable compact discs
- Computers' more central role
- Telecommunications, fax machines, electronic mail

. . . the list goes on.

Here's what I'm saying: As you define what you want, also define how that fits into the world. *Look for problems, not openings.* This strategy will not only help you in your overall job search, but in the interview itself.

LISTEN TO THE MUSIC PLAYING IN YOUR HEAD

You are a collection of skills, values and preferences. (And you thought you were just a lawyer, a professor, a carpenter, a homemaker, a college graduate or a chef.) All of the information you just defined is what constitutes The Job You Want. This information now helps you explain it to other people and will guide you in finding The Job You Want. And since the needs of the world are constantly changing, this information also helps you stay valuable. It allows you to evaluate where your skills and talents fit in as the world changes.

But you do have to stay current on what the world needs and how your talents, experience and interests fit in. Read the paper and listen to the news.

Finally, you will not find happiness in your work if you merely go after a job title or function. You need to pursue all of these elements.

CHECKLIST

✔ To get the job you want, define the job you want.

✔ Write out:

- a list of the skills you will use
- your personal characteristics
- the kind of people you work for
- how much you're paid
- the knowledge you can contribute
- environment
- type of business
- how you will grow and be recognized and where the job could lead

✔ Give yourself time to construct this list.

✔ Believe you have a right to create that picture—and to get that job; you have a right to be happy in your work.

✔ See that picture on paper and you will be closer to getting The Job You Want.

✔ See yourself as a body of skills and talents that can help solve a problem.

✔ Pay attention to trends.

✔ Look for problems, not openings.

CHAPTER 2

You're Here to Save the Day

Strategy #2

**Face it and embrace it:
They want someone who can increase
profits or cut costs.**

Only one person cares that you need or want a job—you.

OK, your mother, spouse, significant other or friends care. But the interviewer doesn't care or want to know how many bills you have, what your mortgage is, that you have a career to build and a 401(k) to fund.

It's not that the interviewer is a heartless, stingy louse. But unless she *is* your mother, she will not hire you simply because you need or want a job. And if you're going to get The Job You Want, you don't want to be hired for those reasons anyway.

We live in a capitalist marketplace that values productivity, efficiency and profit. That bottom-line thinking has intensified as companies continue to cut workers to be more profitable and competitive. The people who are left—or new employees—must justify their existence.

Even though there's discussion about putting people first, the majority of executives still put profits first, according to a 1995 survey by management consultant Towers Perrin Company. (Hey, at least they're talking about putting people first now—ten years ago, no one cared that much about it. Another ten years down the road, when the surplus of workers has diminished, they'll take it more seriously.)

So now, more than ever, the *only* reason someone hires you is because you personally will impact the company's success. You can solve their problems. That's how they'll be more productive, efficient and profitable—and thrive. Specifically, they hire you because you can do one or more of the following:

- Make or deliver their product or service
- Sell their product or service
- Run their operations so they can make, sell and deliver their product or service

These are problems every company faces—whether you work for a hospital, bank, nonprofit organization, dental office, publisher, university, government agency or a shoelace manufacturer.

OVERVIEW OF A TYPICAL COMPANY
People Who Need People

Let's create a fictitious company, Shoes & More Shoes, to illustrate this point. This is an extremely over-simplified explanation so please don't show this to your economics professor from college and say, "Why couldn't you have just told me this?"

To be in business, Shoes & More Shoes must first have a product. But to make it, the company must:

- Determine, locate and purchase materials to make the product
- Research costs
- Schedule and supervise shifts of personnel to make the product
- Create the product
- Package the product for shipment

The above are production problems. The people you find doing this type of work might be in production, purchasing, inventory control, warehousing, management, quality control, supervision, maintenance or new product development.

Once the shoes are ready, the company needs to:

- Develop a plan to get its products to customers
- Attract customers
- Deliver the products
- Keep customers satisfied

The above are sales, marketing and distribution problems. The people doing this type of work are involved in the delivery and sales of the product. They might be in marketing, sales, customer service, advertising, public relations, merchandising, promotion and distribution, traffic and transportation or shipping and receiving.

While all this is going on, other people are making sure everything is running smoothly, bills are being paid and everybody has everything they need to do their jobs. These people:

- Answer phones and handle correspondence
- Order supplies, send out bills, collect money and pay suppliers
- Take orders
- Create procedures and policies

The above are operational and administrative problems. The people who do this work are involved in the operational and administrative parts of the company. They might be in operations, administration, management, accounting, finance or information systems.

To the Rescue

As an employee, you help solve these problems. The better you can do that, the more you will impact the company's success and the happier you will make the boss.

Of course you expect to be compensated with a salary or an hourly wage. The company pays you according to your level of experience and value. It doesn't pay you because you need or want money; it pays you because your skills solve its problems in an efficient and effective manner.

The interviewer is looking for someone with prob-

lem-solving skills that will either increase profits or cut costs. She holds the interview to find out if you've got what it takes. If you are going to get The Job You Want, you must understand and embrace this thinking—the employer's point of view. Then you must show her that you think like her and have what it takes.

OK, test time. Why are you looking for a job?

1. I got laid off from my old one.
2. I need more money than I make now.
3. I have to support my family and pay for our daughter's college.
4. I need more experience and a new opportunity.
5. I'm bored.
6. My parents are kicking me out of the house.
7. I'll go nuts if I stay home another day.
8. I got my degree.
9. I want to contribute my talents, skills and knowledge to make a company more productive and effective in delivering a product or service that I believe in.

I'm sure you picked 9. You picked it, not because it's what the interviewer wants to hear (even though she does), but because you *mean* it. You understand that's why businesses exist and why someone would hire you. Yes, it's what the interviewer is looking for. But so are you. Options 1 through 8 might all be true. But they are not the motivating factors for getting The Job You Want. They are motivating factors for getting *any* job.

If it seems as though I'm beating you over the head with this point, I am. It is the interview strategy that is the foundation for all others. You must understand it. It will be applied to everything else you do.

DIFFERENT STROKES FOR DIFFERENT FOLKS

During a job hunt, you may be interviewed by one or more types of company representatives. Each has his or her own agenda.

Recruiter/Executive Search Firm/Headhunter

These people are hired by a company to find someone to fill an opening because the company doesn't have the time or know-how to recruit employees or feels it's more effective to use an outside source. They are not a clearinghouse for job openings. They are not supposed to help you get a job.

Then what do they do? Most likely, they put your resumé into a database. If your talents and area of specialization are ever needed, you'll get brought up on the screen, and possibly called and interviewed. That's most likely when you'll hear from them—when they need someone to fill a slot.

Get to know recruiters and build relationships with them over the course of your career. If you get a call from one regarding a particular position, be sure to ask how you would work together. Ask what their role is in this relationship.

KEY FUNCTIONS:

• To prescreen you to decide if you have the right skills, knowledge and attitude for the job their client has open.

• To send you for an interview if you are what the hiring company is looking for.

HOW TO TREAT THEM:

Always treat recruiters as if they were the actual employer. Many people think recruiters work for the job hunter. As friendly and helpful as recruiters may seem, treat them like employers. That's who pays them.

When you talk about salary, for example, use your judgment. I tell people to give a range. But some recruiters tell me that if you're not totally open about your salary they won't work with you. Other recruiters will settle for a range. If you do give your exact salary, be sure to also tell them the range you are qualified for. Whatever you do, don't lie.

Let's look more closely at what they do—which affects how you treat them. Assuming you're the right person for the job, yes, they want to do everything they can to get you to accept the position. That's how they make their money. So, acting as the intermediary, they are smart to help you get what you want.

But as much as the recruiter wants to make money, he needs to earn his keep. His first obligation is to the employer—that's who pays him. His duty is to dig up as much information as possible to help the employer decide whether you're the right person for the job.

Once he does that, the headhunter goes back to the employer with whatever he finds out: references, past dates of employment and past salary (if he can get it). The more information the employer has about you, the more advantageous the position he's in.

Since the headhunter's job is to size you up, he'll ask questions that may seem out of the ordinary: Do you own your house? Do you have kids? Does your spouse work? This helps him know whether you fit the specifications that the hiring company has outlined as the perfect match.

One recruiter told me he won't work with you if you don't tell him the information he wants to know. Remember—he's trying to prequalify you. From his side of the table, this saves everyone time. That's why he wants you to be forthright about these "logistical issues."

On the other hand, some questions you could hear could be inappropriate because they have nothing to do with whether you're qualified for the position. If you feel that way about a question, you can respond with "Why do you ask?" or "Why is that relevant?"

You want to develop a positive relationship with headhunters. Just don't forget that most everything you tell them will go right back to the employer. You can be sure that he will at least share the logistical information that determines whether it's even feasible to hire you (whether you have kids, are open to relocation, own your house and so on).

One recruiter summed up his work like this: "I protect the employer from deals that are dead in the water because that's who I work for. If you're the right person, I'll do whatever I can to make the deal happen. If you're not right, I'll do what I have to do to spare everyone agony and expense."

Human Resource or Personnel Director

These people are employees of the hiring company. They tend to be better than average interviewers because this is one their main roles in the organization.

These days they can be called most anything. I've heard of companies who call the head of personnel "Vice President for People" or "Vice President of People Systems."

KEY FUNCTIONS:

• To prescreen you to determine whether you can do what's listed on the job description and fit into the company.

• To decide your fate by determining whether or not you make it to the next round of interviews.

HOW TO TREAT THEM:

• Let them take the lead: Answer their questions politely, giving information that demonstrates you can do the job.

• Don't get into a lot of technical detail about your work—unless they ask. They may not be that familiar with exactly what you do.

Manager or Supervisor

This might be the person you work for. You wind up here because personnel gave you the go-ahead, it's your first contact because you're interviewing in a firm that doesn't have a personnel department, or you were referred to this person.

KEY FUNCTIONS:

• To decide whether you have the right skills and knowledge for the job. (Since he has first-hand experience with the job, he looks more closely at your abilities.)

• To find out how you would handle particular problems—ones he knows you'll face on the job.

• To assess how well you will get along with him and the rest of the staff.

HOW TO TREAT THEM:

• Treat them like a potential employer.

• Stay focused on presenting information that demonstrates your value.

• Stay away from questions about salary or anything that does not support your qualifications to do the job.

Recruiter at a Job Fair

When unemployment is high, it's a buyer's (employer's) market. The lines at job fairs are long and you only have a few minutes to talk to company representatives. If unemployment is low, there may be more companies present than job hunters. You'll have more time to talk—perhaps even enough time to hold an interview.

KEY FUNCTIONS:

• To get first impressions and either set up interviews or collect resumés for a committee back at the office that will decide who to call for interviews.

HOW TO TREAT THEM:

• Smile, have a professional appearance and positive attitude, display good communication skills and confidence.

• Plan your first three sentences. Recruiters rely heavily on first impressions and you may only have a minute or two to meet. Be as likable as you can.

Temporary Agencies

These are companies that establish a pool of employees who can fill a temporary job at a company. They act as the liaison between you and the employer. You sign up with the agency, and when they have a need to fill, they call you.

This is a great way to start on a temporary basis and move to a full-time position. In fact, according to the National Association of Temporary and Staffing Services, 38 percent of the nation's temporary workers say they have been offered a full-time job while on assignment.

People register with temporary agencies to fill the gap between jobs (54 percent of temporary workers are in between jobs).

Many of my clients have learned new software at these firms, since most will test and train you on word processing, graphics and spreadsheet programs (66 percent of temporary employees say they gained new skills during their tenure as a temporary).

Some people even have full-time careers as temporaries. They enjoy working in different companies for short terms.

KEY FUNCTIONS:

• To screen you just as if you are their employee. (In essence, you are. They look for people who are flexible, trainable and professional. The more flexible your schedule, the more apt they are to get you assignments.)

• To take the place of the human resource department of the company they could be sending you to.

Once you've worked for a particular company and

the management likes and needs you, your position could become permanent. So now the company you work for becomes your potential employer. They are looking at your actual performance on the job.

More so than another type of employer, temporary agencies want to get a feel for your overall skills, interests and volunteer activities, and to explore other things you've done. This helps them know what industries or positions you might fit in, be interested in or have exposure to—making you more valuable to their clients.

HOW TO TREAT THEM:

• Treat the people at the temporary agency like a potential employer.

One temporary agency manager told me some people come to her office without dressing up, thinking, "You're not my employer." How wrong they are. That's exactly who she is.

She also said her company likes employees who, once they're on assignment, stay in touch with them to let them know how things are going. If things get rocky, they can help the employee work the problem out or change assignments. Overall, it makes for better relations among all parties involved. Knowing this, you might make a point to mention the importance of open and regular contact with them (the temporary agency).

No matter who you talk to in the *first* round of interviews—recruiter, human resource personnel or a manager—their job is not to hire you. It's to screen you in or out of the process. (I talk about the second and third round in chapter eight.)

And no matter which one of them you talk to, they're all looking for the same thing: the perfect employee. That includes temperament or attitude that fits the job and their company and the skills to do the job. All of this rolled up into one makes you someone who can solve their problems.

INTERVIEWERS SCRUTINIZE FIVE THINGS

Employers read books and go to seminars that warn them of the exorbitant cost to hire and train someone new—between ten thousand and thirty thousand dollars. If they hire the wrong person, it can also cost them tons in terms of productivity and morale—and possibly litigation. So they do everything they can to minimize their risks.

That's why they poke into your past, asking questions of you and people who know you in the hope that they too will know you before they invite you to come on board. It's why they look for clues about whether you're really as good as your resumé says you are. It's why they scrutinize the following areas.

Let's See Your Muscles: What Can You Do?

Every job requires a certain set of functional skills. These are things you actually do, as opposed to what you know. Throughout the book I will refer to these as your *skills and abilities*.

Les, a man in one of my seminars, was a corporate trainer looking for a new job. He knew that the ideal candidate could:

• *Teach* concepts and ideas to adults
• *Facilitate* groups
• *Write* training materials
• *Communicate* effectively
• *Motivate* students to participate

Without these skills, it's highly unlikely he'd be considered for the position. The employer needs to know you're at least qualified to do the job.

If you're going to make it in this extremely competitive, customer-oriented, quality-focused marketplace, you will also need some core skills that are basic to any job. They're called *core workplace competencies*. Now I'm not a big fan of highfalutin', academic-sounding words like that. But I do think they're absolutely, positively imperative for you to know about.

Core workplace competencies are described by Jeanne C. Meister, author of *Corporate Quality Universities*, as the specific skills or know-how that employees need to successfully operate in the workplace, according to the American companies she interviewed.

They include six groups: learning skills, basic skills, interpersonal skills, creative thinking and problem solving, leadership and visioning skills and self-management skills.

"Oh, that stuff—I knew that," you might be saying, your hand already reaching for the next page. Stay with me a minute.

If you said your interpersonal skills were one of your strengths, what do you mean?

"You know, I get along well with people," you might say.

Pretty lame. Here's what *interpersonal skills* means in today's workforce, according to Meister: "Knowing how to listen and communicate with co-workers and customers, resolve conflicts constructively, negotiate and, importantly, network inside and outside the organization."

What if you said you were a leader? What does that mean? Or you said you had vision . . . can you define it? When I probe people to define their leadership skills, most of them say anything from "I can motivate people to get the job done" to "I can take charge of groups to get things done." They usually have a tough time with vision.

According to Meister, *leadership and visioning* are "being able to empower co-workers and 'envision, energize and enable' a group or team to achieve the corporation's business initiatives. Knowing how to value a diverse workforce and importantly, how to recognize co-workers in a timely and appropriate fashion for a job well done."

This particular skill is so important, I want to share some other points of view.

The Chinese philosopher, Lao Tzu, in *Tao Te Ching*, says this about the qualities of a leader: "The leader acts with little motion, instructs not with words but by deeds, keeps informed but seldom interferes. The leader is a teacher who succeeds without taking credit. And because credit is not taken, credit is received."

How do you do that?

You don't necessarily have to be the most charismatic, persuasive person in the world to be a good leader. Mary Anne Devanna, co-author of *The Transformational Leader*, said that, "leaders can quietly inspire through other means such as technical ability, insight and honesty."

Good leaders understand how other people feel, what makes them tick and how to influence them. If you want to see leadership in action, rent the movie *Gettysburg*. There's a scene, early in the film, in which actor Jeff Daniels, playing the role of Major Chamberlain, has been notified that 120 mutineers from his home state of Maine have been assigned to his regiment. He must march into battle while guarding them. If they don't cooperate, he is authorized to shoot them. From his treatment of them when they arrive to his speech to them where he explains the challenges they will all face in battle the next day, his leadership is so convincing that they set aside their grievances and join his troops in battle.

Learning skills are "knowing how to understand and manipulate new information quickly and confidently . . . showing a commitment to self-development and constantly improving one's ability to learn new skills and competencies." I don't remember seeing that kind of language in very many job descriptions before.

One more that is definitely a sign of the times is *self-development* or *self-management skills*, defined as: "Having the ability to proactively manage one's own development and career, rather than to just passively follow a training plan laid out by one's manager."

Basic skills are reading, writing and mathematical computations you need to handle the increased demands of all jobs.

Creative thinking and problem-solving skills are "knowing how to recognize and define problems, implement solutions and track and evaluate results. Above all, possessing the cognitive reasoning skills necessary to transcend sequential thinking and leap to creative solutions."

I'm not suggesting you regurgitate these words in a job interview so you'll sound like hot stuff. I am suggesting you examine their meaning and how they apply to your career. Redefine your strengths in this new language.

Companies have different expectations of you than they used to. You're expected to do more, expand your role, learn other jobs in the company, take initiative and handle conflicts. That's what the basic requirements—these core competencies—reflect.

Remember, these core skills would be in addition to the specific technical skills I described above that are unique to each position. (You'd think I'd get tired of coming up with things for you to do.)

OK, Flex 'Em: How Do You Apply Yourself?

You can have all the right functional skills, but the wrong attitude. Every job requires a set of *personal characteristics and attitudes* that show you're willing to do what it takes to be successful. The company determines what those are and will watch and listen closely for evidence that you possess them.

For example, important personal characteristics for a sales representative might be enthusiasm, sincerity, persuasiveness, empathy, determination and persistence. These personal characteristics, or ways you apply yourself, are sometimes subtly conveyed and in the smallest ways.

Other times, people are not so subtle. A man came to me because he was let go from his position and had not been able to land a new job. I described the process we would go through and what each step would accomplish.

He described himself as a patient, flexible, open and accepting person. At every meeting, he would tap on the table and say, "So, where is this getting me?" He interrupted when I spoke. He sat with his arms crossed in front of him. He held his head slightly cocked and in a way that he always looked down at me. Does he sound patient and flexible to you?

The attitude he conveyed through words and body language was that he was demanding, impatient, inflexible and condescending. Can you guess why he lost his job and why he's having trouble finding a new one?

Laurie, a young woman who had just graduated from college, came to me because she couldn't figure out why she was having so much trouble getting a job. She seemed confident and poised. She stated that she was decisive and focused and knew exactly what she wanted. When I asked what that was, she listed five completely different areas.

After we talked awhile, I said, "You sound as if you're not sure what you want."

"I know what I want. I mean I think I do. I thought I did . . . maybe I don't."

Now I was seeing the real person. And if I had been an employer, I would have lost interest.

This is what you often hear referred to as "fit." It can be difficult to put your finger on, but an interviewer can sense when the fit with the company or job just isn't there.

Although various jobs stress some characteristics over others, it's safe to say that most companies would like your attitude to demonstrate enthusiasm, flexibility, commitment, integrity and confidence, and that you be results- and team-oriented and cus-

tomer-focused. In addition, because the workplace has changed so drastically, they will look for other characteristics I cover at the end of this chapter.

Open Wide: How Do You Sound?

Employers want to hear what comes out when the words start to flow—*your ability to communicate.* You hear this so often you might be tempted to minimize its importance. Or because you've gotten this far in life you figure, "of course I can communicate."

The ability to communicate does not mean that you can string words together into sentences that come out when you open your mouth. It means that you exchange information and express ideas effectively so there is meaning in the exchange between you and another person. It's a process that helps people learn what someone one else thinks and feels.

Why is this ability so important? Communication is the essence of every relationship. Your communication skills—displayed verbally and through the written word—affect customers, clients and other employees, which in turn affect the success of the company. These skills are so important to the interview process that chapters six and seven deal solely with communications.

What Do You Have to Show for Yourself: What Makes You So Good?

Although you have already proven yourself at your present or past jobs and through your experiences, the only thing a new employer has to go on is your *potential*, which is based on your past. To employers, your past is evidence of how you'll act in the future.

Employers see potential in ways you have made past employers profitable or how you've been productive and efficient in your work as a student or in volunteer positions. You'll learn more about how to demonstrate this potential in chapter seven.

I Don't Know, Kid, Something Just Doesn't Seem Right: What About Fit?

You can have it all and still . . . there's just something about you. It's hard to put into words. The interviewer just doesn't feel right about you. *How an interviewer feels about you* is just what it is. Sometimes things don't click. It's almost undefinable. The chemistry is not there. For some reason the interviewer is hesitant about you. Logical or not, interviewers listen to their gut.

QUE SERA, SERA?

"Whatever will be will be . . . the future's not ours to see . . ." might have been good advice once. But today, when it comes to your career you need to examine what the futurists are predicting, where the trends are moving and the characteristics and qualities employers want now and for the future.

Then fill in your gaps. Are you up to speed on the latest developments in your field? Become computer literate if you're not already. Most secretaries and office support personnel must be computer literate; the majority of middle and senior managers need to be computer literate. Companies will hire older workers, but you must be flexible, open to new ideas and up on the latest technology.

Don't wait to be told what your career options are. Don't expect someone else to design your career path.

Things aren't what they used to be. A need to compete in an international market, lifestyle changes and consumer demands have changed the dynamics of working relationships and the way business is conducted. Here are a few examples of how the marketplace has changed:

THE OLD WAYS	THE NEW WAYS
Managers managed.	Employees lead.
People sought security.	People seek ways to stay valuable in a changing market.
Since the middle of the century, successful people went to school, got a job, and stayed there until retirement.	People change jobs and careers several times.
Until the 1980s, the percentage of the population working for large companies has continued to go up.	In the last ten to fifteen years, the trend has been moving toward small companies; 97 percent of companies in the United States have fewer than one hundred employees.

THE OLD WAYS	THE NEW WAYS
Between 1925 and 1975, most big companies were bureaucratic, grew slowly and rewarded the status quo.	Growing companies encourage experimentation and risk taking and value the entrepreneur.
The workforce was mostly white males.	The majority of the workforce is women and minorities.*

Yesterday Life Was Such an Easy Game to Play

As this shift continues, so will a company's expectations of its workers. To create a fulfilling, financially fruitful career and be valued (employed) as we move into the twenty-first century, you need to be more than you were yesterday.

Today Employers Expect You To:

- Know yourself, your strengths and values
- Always look for new ways to contribute and take responsibility for your career path
- Cope with uncertainty and change
- Understand and appreciate diversity among people
- Be willing to try new approaches
- Be willing to wear several hats
- Know how to use computers
- Be service-oriented
- Appreciate the importance of and have good people skills
- Understand how the international marketplace can affect your particular business (it also helps to know other languages and cultures)
- Be self-motivated and confident
- Be willing to take risks
- Be dedicated to growing and seek continued education
- Be willing to work on teams
- Have high standards and strive to be number one
- Have sound ethical judgment

*According to the U.S. Department of Labor Statistics, in 1964, 41 percent of the workforce was made up of women and minorities (non-white males); in 1994, 54 percent of the workforce was made up of women and minorities.

Plus These Good Old-fashioned Ones

These basic personal characteristics will never go out of style. Employees who:

- Are willing to work hard
- Are quality minded
- Get along with others
- Are reliable
- Do whatever it takes to get the job done
- Have a pleasant personality
- Are excited about their work
- Have integrity
- Are open to criticism
- Help others

SUMMARY

Whether you're interviewing for a job as a systems analyst, editor, nurse, quality manager or environmentalist, interviewers look for the same thing. They want to know if you can solve the problems they face in order to:

- Make or deliver their product or service
- Sell their product or service
- Run their operations so they can make, sell and deliver their product or service

They want to hear that because of you, the organization will be more productive, efficient and profitable, and will thrive in an increasingly competitive, service-oriented, quality-minded international market. Your job is to prove it by tuning in to what they care about most.

Today employers are most likely to hire people who work well in a group and bring a spirit of enthusiasm.

But if you work on communicating these points because you think it's what the interviewer wants to hear, you're missing the point of how to get The Job You Want.

Yes, you need to speak the interviewer's language, understand why businesses exist and why someone would hire you. But those are also the motivating factors for getting The Job You Want: To contribute your talents, skills and knowledge to make a company more productive and effective in delivering a product or service that *you* believe in.

CHECKLIST

Show employers you:

- ✔ Have the talents and skills required for the job
- ✔ Have the attitudes that show you're willing to do what it takes to be successful (good fit)
- ✔ Have effective communication skills
- ✔ Have potential to help make the company more profitable
- ✔ Are likable

CHAPTER 3

Tiptoe Through the Tulips

Strategy #3

**Concentrate on one thing:
getting invited to the interview.**

Both you and the company can tell a lot more about each other in the flesh.

But the company has the upper hand at this point. It will decide whether you come through its doors or not. So your goal now is *to be invited to an interview*. This chapter will cover ways they can check you out before they meet you and how you can avoid giving them a reason to screen you out.

We are going to assume there is either a known opening that you are interested in or the company has some interest in you because of a future need.

What other kinds of situations are there? Well, you never know. Because you're out there doing everything I told you to do—staying updated on recent developments in your field and paying close attention to trends, problems and needs in the changing world—you get an idea of how your skills and interests fill a need and can solve problems. So you're talking to decision makers in companies and shazam! You create a position for yourself. It could happen.

But for our discussion here, I'll be talking about how to get invited to an interview for a position that exists and is—or will be—open.

You might be one of hundreds, even thousands of people who responds to a job opening. People hear about jobs through:

- An advertisement in the newspaper
- A friend, neighbor or associate who works at the company or knows someone there
- A job bank listing in a professional journal
- A recruiter

- A posting on The Net (the electronic medium that links millions of computers)

Most of the people who respond won't get interviews. They'll get screened out by an individual, or by a committee of people looking for the top five candidates. The more enlightened a company's management is about hiring practices, the more thorough it will be in these pre-interview screening techniques.

What are they looking for? You guessed it: In essence, whether you have the skills and knowledge to do the job and the right attitude. Here's how they will try to establish that before they go to the expense of interviewing you.

SCREEN TESTS
Cover Letters and Resumés

THEY SCREEN FOR:
- Experience that shows you can do the job
- Attitudes that demonstrate your fit with the company
- Evidence that they will benefit if they hire you

HOW TO PASS:
- In your cover letter, tell them why they'd want to talk to you: You have the potential to increase profits or reduce costs. Give a few examples.
- Focus on what you can do for them, not what they can do for you.
- List achievements—with emphasis on results—on your resume.
- Don't bring up your problems (that you're look-

ing for a job or ways to further your career). Here is an example of what I'm talking about. This is the opening of a letter in response to an advertised position:

Dear Ms. Fritz:

The job you have open for Director of Nurse Recruiting seems to be the next logical step in my career.

It may seem fine, but it conveys the wrong attitude. Companies don't hire you because of what's logical or good for your career. The opening sentence of the letter, which dictates whether or not the reader will go on, has a "what you can do for me" tone. A better approach:

Dear Ms. Fritz:

You mentioned several things in your advertisement for Director of Nurse Recruiting that indicate you may be looking for someone with my background and expertise.

The changes seem subtle, but the result could be the difference between your letter landing an interview or landing in the trash.

Job Applications

THEY SCREEN FOR:
- Information your resumé didn't provide

Many job hunters—especially those in more senior positions—ask me if they have to complete every application. "Can't I just attach a resumé?" Not unless the application says you can. Here's why.

When someone becomes my client, I give him or her forms to complete. I ask for data that in some cases is on the resumé. But I want the information recorded on *my* form for two reasons: (1) if the information is listed in the format I request, it saves hours of time when we rewrite the resumé and (2) most of the time, the old resumé doesn't have the information I need. So I want my clients to follow the directions stated on my form.

Inevitably, someone returns the forms with a note on the blank page: "See attached resumé." This is almost always a red flag. For example, Pete was one of those clients who didn't follow directions. He turned out to be one of the most controlling and

uncooperative people I've ever met. Bottom line: His attitude stinks. I promise you—companies will see the same red flag. If you can't follow directions now, employers will wonder, what kind of employee will you be?

- Your answers to questions

These can also be a dead giveaway. For example, most applications ask about past employment and why you left. I've seen responses such as: "The company was stupid when it came to finances, the management made bad decisions, so the company went bankrupt." Trust me on this, too—the applicant probably didn't get an interview.

HOW TO PASS:
- Get sample applications from a business supply store.

Write your responses to questions and show them to someone who can objectively tell you what your attitude conveys.

- If the application asks what kind of salary you want to make, write "Open."

Telephone

Although the company representative might be calling to set an appointment, let's assume he's conducting a phone interview first to see if he wants to meet you.

THEY SCREEN FOR:
- Whether you pass the basic job requirements

These may include your willingness and availability to travel, relocate or work a particular shift or whether you have the necessary certification or degree.

- Clues about the five things employers scrutinize that I covered in chapter two

He'll ask questions such as: Could you tell me more about yourself? What kind of position are you looking for? What's your background? Why do you want to leave your company? Why did you leave? What kind of salary are you looking for?

See what you can find out about the position. Ask about job title, responsibilities and qualifications for the job. This will help you prepare for the interview.

Your only goal at this point: To be invited in for an interview.

HOW TO PASS:

- Make a great impression with the only thing you've got when you're on the phone—your voice.

Be polite. Listen to questions. Don't interrupt. Be enthusiastic. Smile—it comes through in your voice.

- Give brief answers to questions.

Say, "I'd be happy to tell you more about that when we meet." Tantalize him so he'll *want* to meet. You can be much more effective in person.

I'll go into detail on how to handle the question of salary during the interview in chapter ten. If you are asked about salary in this phase, skirt the issue. It's irrelevant and only being asked to screen you in or out of the interview process. You want to be considered for a position because you're qualified, not because of what you want to be paid.

If asked, say: "I don't know much about the position you have open, so it would be difficult to talk about salary at this point." If he persists, come back with: "I don't feel comfortable talking about salary on the telephone. Could we meet and learn more about each other to decide if there's a good fit? It seems as if it would make sense to talk about salary then." You can add: "I'm sure you offer a competitive salary."

If he's really pushy, as a last resort, give a range.

The reason I want you to ask questions about the position is so you can decide if it is a position you want to consider. If you have a feel for the job, you'll have some feel for the salary.

It doesn't hurt if *they* offer salary information. Early in my career, I received a call from the personnel director at a company in response to an ad I answered. The very first thing she said was, "This job pays $15,000. If that's not suitable, there's no point in coming in for an interview." This information helped me know that I had applied for the wrong position and would be wasting their time *and* mine.

On the other hand, if they mention the salary range for a position that does interest you, store it away as data to use during salary negotiations.

- Take notes on what he says.

One more thing: If he calls when you're just stepping out of the shower, changing a diaper, having dinner or the dog is barking, ask him if you can call right back. You can't hold an intelligent conversation under any of these circumstances. You'll be distracted, it will come through in your voice, and you'll end up sounding disinterested or scatterbrained.

References

THEY SCREEN FOR:

- The undesirables

I once read that one-fifth of job applicants lie on their resumés, cover letters and applications. Employers have also read this statistic, so they *will* check your references. If they're really thorough, they do this before they even call you.

HOW TO PASS:

- Contact the people you want to use as references *before* you give their name out.

Make sure they agree to be a reference and will share the kind of information that will help, not hurt you. (In chapter four I talk about how to coach and follow up with references.)

The owner of a printing company told me he was looking for a salesperson and wanted to check out an applicant before he flew her into town for an interview. When he called one of her references, this person shared only derogatory information about her. It turns out the applicant had an affair with the reference's husband.

Someone else who I have known professionally for several years called me after his job had been eliminated and told (not asked) me to expect a call because he used me as a reference. He didn't know I found out several months prior to the call that he had lied about some information. Because of that incident, I did not feel comfortable being a reference.

Let's say there's someone you want to have as a reference, but you haven't had much contact for several years. Write her a note to re-establish your relationship. Then follow up with a phone call. In the future, don't wait until you need someone to connect with them.

Videoconferencing

If an employer has the equipment, he can sit in his office and "meet" you on a 27-inch television screen or on the desktop version of his computer. This is called videoconferencing.

It's a technique used by nearly half the largest U.S. corporations to conduct business with their offices across the country (and across the continents), to team up with other professionals to solve a problem, or to talk to customers, suppliers and subcontractors.

Now it's made its way into the interview process. Recruiters and employers may use it to screen you because it's a lot cheaper than flying you into town; most likely, you would go to a nearby videoconferencing site.

If you're graduating from college, this may be the way an employer will interview you, thanks to universities that are installing InterVIEW—a version of this interactive videoconferencing. It's still very new, but catching on quickly (in 1995, eighty-nine universities across the country offered this interviewing option; only two offered it in 1994).

Basically, the system has created a more convenient way for employers to link up with students and is a much cheaper route than sending recruiters to your campus. Some public and private university career centers have created consortiums to offer this service. The Southeastern and Atlantic Coast University Electronic Career Network, or SEACnet, is one.

Here's how it works:

- If your school is a member, you go to your career services office, where you register and become part of the electronic database.
- Employers contact the career center, saying something like: We're looking for an engineer with a 3.5 grade average, who has done this and that and can do that and this, someone who knows all about whatnots and will be available on such-and-such a date.
- The people at the career center put this information into their database, which then spits out the candidates' resumés that fit the criteria ("download" is the correct technical jargon). They then send those names and resumés to the employer.
- If the employer wants to interview you, he can always do so in person or via telephone. But if he wants to cut costs and get a feel for you, videoconferencing is a way to do it. Let's say he does want to meet you via video. He sets up a videoconference time with your school. (There's a schedule on the Internet that tells them when they can do that—it's like signing up for usage of a conference room.)
- If the employer has compatible equipment he can sit right there in his office and interview you. Otherwise, he goes to the nearest university site or compatible videoconferencing site.
- You show up at your university's videoconferencing site the day of the interview and, just like magic, you can both see and hear each other. You can also "look" at your resumé together and transmit or receive data.

Now, this will take some getting used to. When you first see each other, your movements look a bit jerky and stilted. But there is no lag time after you say something—so it doesn't seem like you're talking to somebody on the space shuttle. Also, your facial expressions will come through loud and clear. But remember to look at the camera when you speak; if you don't, your eyes look closed.

You'll probably see more of this taking place around the world as more companies get the equipment.

THEY SCREEN FOR:
- How you look, how you sit, your clothes, if you look friendly and confident.
- How you answer questions.

HOW TO PASS:
- Sit in a comfortable chair. (Don't slouch or look too stiff. Be natural.)
- Wear a conservative suit.
- Smile.
- Be conversational.

Videoconferencing Online

This is the next step up from just plain videoconferencing. It's where you and the employer can both just sit in front of your computers and talk. Neither of you has to go to a videoconferencing site (and you can even wear jeans if you want).

You have to have the right equipment: a powerful computer, fast Internet connection and the correct multicasting software. This is still quite new, but it's a significant development. Expect to see a lot more of this within the next two years as more people learn about it and the technology improves—and the price goes down.

Tip:
Move slowly because you will look very jerky—even if you're just sitting quietly.

TESTS
Some companies conduct tests before they interview you to:

- Determine how successful you'll be on the job
- Determine how well you'll work in their environment and culture
- Eliminate you if you just have a talent for acing interviews

Tests are usually the best predictor of how well someone will do on the job, so many companies rely on them. How much credence does a company put in test results? Based on the results, they could decide not to interview you.

THEY SCREEN FOR (DEPENDING ON YOUR JOB):
- *Intelligence*—your capacity to acquire and apply knowledge
- *Skills*—what you already know
- *Aptitude*—your capacity to learn other skills
- *Interests*—what you'll most likely enjoy doing
- *Attitude*—how you tend to act or approach things

HOW TO PASS:
- Agree to take tests without flinching. This probably wouldn't be your first reaction. Most people—even those who feel they do well on tests—react with hesitation, wondering, "What is the company trying to find out?" (And it shows.) If you want to pursue the position, you have to take the tests. So when the company says it wants to do testing, say, "I'd be happy to."

- Generally, the company wants you to feel comfortable. But they might be observing how you react during the test. Someone whose job it is to administer tests told me it is also part of his duties to record how applicants outwardly exhibit their feelings while taking tests. If you've ever taken tests, you've probably felt frustrated at times, having to pick from limited choices that may not accurately describe you. Other times you can feel pressured to give the right answer in a short time period. If it's a written test, don't throw down the pencil or look exasperated. Big brother could be watching.

- Don't expect to answer all the questions—especially if you've been given a limited time to complete them. If you don't know an answer, go to the next question.

- Don't manipulate the test by trying to figure out what it's attempting to determine. If you don't do well on a test, you don't want to work in that job anyway and you could be getting in over your head.

- Understand the directions and requirements of the test. For example, some tests penalize you for guessing, while others give you credit for guessing if you don't know an answer. So, depending on the test, if you run out of time at the end it might help or hurt you to just fill in the blanks. If the person administering the test doesn't tell you this information, ask.

- Prepare by taking practice tests. Check your bookstore for references that have sample tests. Most people aren't accustomed to taking exams; brush up on your vocabulary, math and comprehensive skills.

- A word on lie detector tests: According to the Employee Polygraph Protection Act of 1988, you can refuse to take a lie detector test. But government agencies, some private sector employers (such as drug companies and private security firms), and positions that affect national security or that involve law enforcement are exempt under this act.

BEHIND THE CURTAINS
If you make it past the screening, they'll call you to meet face-to-face. I'll talk about what you can encounter in the next chapter. In the meantime, behind the scenes, they've probably been busy developing a job description that lists:

- Skills, experience, education or training, and attitudes they'd like their ideal candidate to have
- Purpose of the job, expectations and responsibilities
- Compensation

They've also probably developed a list of questions that depend on the job and who is interviewing you. Chapter nine deals with these questions.

If you don't pass this round, expect a "Thanks, but no thanks" letter or phone call. Assuming you played your cards right, however, expect a call to set up your first interview with the company.

SUMMARY

Employers don't like to hire the wrong person. It's expensive, unproductive and potentially demoralizing for everyone. So before they meet you, they're looking for reasons to eliminate you from the interview process. Don't give them one. Otherwise, you may never have the chance to evaluate *them*.

CHECKLIST

✔ Follow directions to the *T* when completing job applications.

✔ Don't be negative, critical or defensive in answering application questions.

✔ Make the most of the only thing you've got when you're on the telephone—your voice. Be pleasant and enthusiastic, and keep answers brief and chock-full of relevant information. Don't talk about salary.

✔ Check with people you want to use as references before you give out their names. Make sure they will say positive things about you.

✔ Agree to take tests without flinching. Don't exhibit frustration during the test.

CHAPTER 4

You're Off to See the Wizard

Strategy #4

**Arm yourself with information
about yourself and the company.**

You did everything right and got the interview. Now it's time to do everything you can to prepare for it. Putting time and effort into the front end will help you accomplish five things:

1. Be ready for the vigilant interviewer whose observant ears and eyes don't miss a thing during the interview.
2. Get paid what you're worth.
3. Present yourself in the best possible light.
4. Demonstrate your understanding of the employer's point of view.
5. Get information to help you evaluate whether this is The Job You Want.

CLIMB EVERY MOUNTAIN, SEARCH HIGH AND LOW

Research (I heard that moan) tends to be one of most job hunters' least favorite activities. By research, I don't necessarily mean you need to spend hours at the library. But before you go to an interview, you do need to know at the very least:

- What the company does
- Who runs the company: names, titles and their philosophies
- Brief company history
- Financial status and sales volume, if applicable

If you're really on your toes, in some cases you'll know more than the interviewer about the company.

It's hard to believe that someone wouldn't research a company prior to applying or interviewing. But many people don't. Once I was sitting in the lobby of a company waiting for an appointment. A young man dropped off a resumé with the receptionist. As he was leaving, he turned back and said, "By the way, what do you do here?"

SOURCES
It's Free and Yours for the Asking

I can't think of too many things that are free, except information. Yes, it will cost you in terms of your time (if you drive to and from the library), long distance charges for phone calls, and the cost of a book or magazine if you buy one. But information on just about anything is easily accessible—in books, on computers and through people—if you know where and how to look for it. And you will more than double your investment of time with the results the search brings.

Annual Reports

Annual reports are available for public companies (and some private firms); call the company for a copy if your library doesn't have one. The information is invaluable.

For instance, let's say you have an interview with Hershey Foods Corporation. Just by reading the first page of their annual report, you would know they are the "leading North American manufacturer of high-quality chocolate and other confectionery products and the leading domestic producer of branded, dry pasta products."

You would know their goals, what new products they introduced in the Canadian market, who they signed new licensing agreements with and that they introduced their products into the Russian market in late 1994.

You can get a sense of their priorities, management philosophy and commitment to issues such as quality and growth. The report reads: "We've had to change our organizational structure to reduce the cycle time required to get new products to market. By utilizing electronic imaging systems and drawing upon the efficiencies of our supplier partnerships, we have dramatically cut the time required to design and produce new packaging."

Chamber of Commerce Directories

Most cities that have a Chamber of Commerce publish a directory of its members listing company principals, date company was founded, number of employees and products or services. You can purchase one from the Chamber or check your library.

These directries can be especially helpful if you're looking for a job in another city. You can find out who the major employers are, information on international business conducted in that city and general data about future development, retailers, education and culture—important factors when considering a geographical move.

Stockbrokers

If you have a relationship with a stockbroker, he or she can tell you what a company does, what percentage of business is international, its most popular products, if it had a recent downsizing, acquisitions and, if it's a public company, about its stock. Otherwise, check *Standard & Poor's* or some of the other references I list. That's one of the places stockbrokers look.

Business Directories

Your library will most likely have a variety of reference books that list companies, associations, schools, hospitals, consultants and trade associations. If you don't know where to look for something, there's even a book called *The Directory of Directories*. Ask librarians for help; they are very knowledgeable and like to help people.

People Who Work at the Company

Employees know what goes on inside the company better than anyone. If you know someone who works in the organization, ask him about the organization's goals, culture, environment and priorities. If you know someone who knows someone who works there, ask the person you know for a referral to that person.

Company Newsletter or Brochures

This is a good place to get insight into the philosophy and to learn who the company does business with, who works there and how it promotes its employees. Call the company's public relations department and ask them to send you what they have.

Articles in the Local Business Papers and National Publications

Go to the business department of your local library for access to articles about the company you're researching. Most libraries nowadays have electronic indexes that make this simple.

For example, the public library in Cincinnati, Ohio, has one database listing eight hundred economic, trade and industry journals and newspapers and some complete articles. This is where you get nuggets of information such as quotes from the company president that tell you its goals, problems and future plans. A service called Newsdex has more than a million local news stories from papers. If you have a computer and modem at home, you can just dial up the information.

The Net

Let's see if I, the least technologically inclined person on Earth, can explain to you, probably more high-tech savvy than me, what this is. If you're like my father, who has stood no closer than four feet from a computer in his life, you'll be impressed.

This definition is based on interviews I've conducted with authors who write books on the subject, two books I've thumbed through on the subject, and conversations I've had with people who do understand it.

"The Net" is the medium that links millions of computers around the world in order to electronically share information. It's also called the "Information Highway." It's also known as "Cyberspace." It encompasses the Internet and online commercial services (commercial means you pay for them). The most popular services are CompuServe (800-848-

8199), America Online (800-827-6465), Prodigy (800-Prodigy), eWorld (800-775-4556) and GEnie (800-638-9636).

That's the definition. For more information, read books like *Be Your Own Headhunter Online* by Pam Dixon and Sylvia Tiersten, and Joyce Lain Kennedy's books *Electronic Job Search Revolution* and *Hook Up, Get Hired!*

Since this section is on the kind of information you can learn about a company, let's get back to that. Once you're "online" (you do that by subscribing to an online service), you can find this kind of information:

- Financial and operational data
- The most socially responsible companies
- The largest and fastest-growing companies
- Sales figures, product lines and gross sales
- CEO and CFO salaries
- Descriptions of company history and culture, future goals and recent stock prices
- International companies

Employers constantly tell me how impressed they are when an applicant has gone to the trouble to research their company.

But don't research to impress them. Sure, you want to research things that demonstrate your interest in the company. But read up on the firm to educate yourself so you can have an informed discussion.

Also, conduct research to help you evaluate the job and the company. Besides the things I've already mentioned, think about what else is important to you—everything from on-site child care, elder care, flex time and job sharing to how it treats women, minorities and gays. Some of this information will be available in the sources I've listed.

WORTH ONE'S SALT

Remember that one element of The Job You Want is to be paid what you're worth. To get what you're worth, you need to know what it is, or you could end up making a lot less. So you need to research your salary.

It's not that employers are trying to cheat you. But they are businesspeople who, for the most part, want to get the most for the least amount of money.

Your goal is to give the most and get paid the highest amount.

What's the highest amount? Whatever is fair and competitive for the job you do. A range already exists for the kind of job you do or the field you're entering. Where you fit into that range will depend on:

- How experienced you are
- How much responsibility you'll have

The more you have of these two things—experience and responsibility—the more valuable you are.

Equal Pay for Equal Work?

Let's talk briefly about salaries between the sexes.

The good news (at least in 1995*): Women in higher level jobs are doing much better than previously reported, taking home eighty to ninety cents for every dollar made by a man in the same position. It's hardly pay equity, but it's an improvement over the situation for working women as a whole, whose average earnings are still just 72 percent of what men earn. Women in a few professions—college administrators, female student deans and chief financial officers—actually earned more than their male counterparts.

The bad news: For married women, in a two-income family, the women may be gaining, but their spouses may be losing. A 1993 survey of 231 married men who received MBAs in the late 1970s found that men who had stay-at-home wives earned 24 percent more over a six-year period and rose to higher management levels than men with working wives. A 1994 study of 348 male managers at twenty Fortune 500 companies found that over a five-year period the men with homemaker wives received raises 20 percent higher than those of men with working wives.

The National Committee on Pay Equity in Washington, DC, works to eliminate sex- and race-based wage discrimination and to achieve pay equity. For more information, call (202) 822-7304.

Working Woman, salary survey, January 1995.

Where to Get Salary Data

BOOKS

The public library has books such as *American Salaries and Wages Survey*, *Geographic Reference Report* and *Occupational Outlook Handbook* that give annual salaries for occupations.

SALARY SURVEYS

These are conducted annually by trade publications and magazines. For example, every January *Working Woman* magazine prints the results of its national salary survey. It also breaks out the figures by gender.

Trade associations also conduct salary surveys. For example, Professional Secretaries International is a group that polls its members. You can call trade associations directly and ask if they have this information.

PEERS

Conduct your own survey of people in your field or the one you want to join. Start with people you know in the industry and ask them to refer you to other people to hold an informational meeting. In these meetings, you can ask questions to gather data about the industry in general, and include salary in your discussion.

Talking about money is always a touchy subject, so I wouldn't flat out ask someone, "How much do you make?" Say something like: "What is the salary range for this profession?"

ONLINE

Join a public discussion group or bulletin board service on the Internet where you can post notes and queries about salary. Your questions are often answered by people in the field. America Online, Jobnet and eWorld also offer career information.

Once you know what the salary range is for a profession, you are equipped to negotiate for the salary you want. (I discuss this in chapter ten.)

COACH YOUR TEAM

Just because you have your references' permission to use their names, you're not done yet. When was the last time you worked with these people? Do they really know your strengths? Are they going to re-

member why you're so great? Remember, they've been busy with their own lives and careers. Update them on your background, qualifications and career objective. Specifically:

- Send them a new resumé and a list of your strengths.
- Tell them your career objective and why you're looking for a job.
- Remind them of the success of the project(s) or program(s) you worked on together.
- If you know, tell them which companies will be calling.
- Tell them you'll follow up (and make sure you do).

They will appreciate the update, plus their input will be consistent with what you say about yourself in the interview. If you know that an employer checked one of your references, call the reference and asked how the conversation went. Thank your reference and keep the person updated.

THE RIGHT INTERVIEW ATTITUDE: DEDICATED TO THE ONE WHO SIGNS THE CHECKS

The right interview attitude conveys your enjoyment in solving problems to increase profits or cut costs. It gives the clear message that you're dedicated to discovering and then doing what you can do for the company. You demonstrate this attitude in several ways.

The Answers You Give

For example, if you're asked, "Why do you want to work for our company?" which answer do you think illustrates the right attitude?

1. I have a cousin who works here and I heard you treat people real well and have good benefits.
2. I'm looking for an opportunity to learn the restaurant business so that someday I can have my own place.
3. I'm looking for an opportunity to learn the consumer products industry.
4. In the research I conducted, I learned that you want to secure more licensing agreements in the international market. I also came across the fact that your goal is to be number one in

pasta products. With my strong background in international sales and successful track record in the food industry, I feel confident I can help you achieve those goals. I particularly enjoy researching new markets. Your company also has an excellent reputation for being responsive to customers' needs through several of the software programs you've developed. Strengthening customer relationships is going to be one of the keys to success in this business and it's something I believe in strongly. I want to work for a company that values its customers as much as I do.

Answers 1 through 3, which focus only on what the company can do for you, do not demonstrate the right attitude. Remember, companies don't give you a job to ensure good treatment and great benefits. They aren't in business to teach you everything you need to know to start your own company or learn a new industry.

Obviously, answer 4 supports the appropriate interview attitude. But that kind of answer won't just pop into your head. You'll need to do your research and have a sense of where you fit into the overall goals of the company.

You'll have plenty opportunities to show that you are a problem solver as you answer other questions during the interview. (I talk more about these questions in chapter nine.)

The Questions You Ask

If you are inclined to ask questions about salary and benefits—don't. That demonstrates a "what can you do for me" attitude. Questions that demonstrate the right attitude have to do with the company and the responsibilities of the job. They also help you appraise your fit. A perceptive interviewer will pick up on your desire to have a mutually satisfying relationship. These questions might include:

- What are the responsibilities of this job?
- What types of problems would I face?
- Who would I report to?
- What are the expectations of the position?
- Would I manage or supervise anyone?
- Why is this position open?
- What does the ideal candidate for this position look like?

- What is a typical day or week like?
- How does this position contribute to the company's goals, productivity or profits?
- How do you evaluate performance?

Questions That Help You Know What's What

Sure, the elements of The Job You Want may vary from someone else's. But every worker I've met wants to work for a company that respects and trusts him or her to do the best job possible. When that trust exists, you are more likely to be motivated, loyal and hard-working.

The key is to ask questions to determine if the company puts a priority on valuing its employees. Some of these questions may get you thinking about others.

- What are the company's long-term goals? How do your employees fit into achieving them?
- What are your customer service philosophy, mission, management and leadership style and values?
- How do you build a national and international reputation?
- How do you recognize your employees for their contributions?

Don't be afraid to ask questions. A young man who was having a tough time getting a new job because he was shy and didn't ask questions during interviews once wrote to me. "Even my current boss almost didn't give me my job because he said I didn't ask questions in the interview," he said.

I suggested he start seeing himself as a confident communicator. To do this, begin in small ways:

- Strike up a conversation with a waiter in a restaurant.
- Speak up more with friends.
- Before the next interview, develop a list of five questions to ask or points to discuss.
- Practice asking the questions on a tape recorder or in front of a mirror.

Hold Your Tongue

I don't care if this is the second or third interview, until you've got an offer, don't ask about pay, benefits, child care and flex time, or potentially sensitive questions such as "How many women or minorities sit on your board or are in senior management?" A better way to ask would be: "How have women progressed at the company?"

As I said earlier, research this information on your own. It can be found in specific sources, such as *The Job Seekers' Guide To Socially Responsible Companies.* It profiles about one thousand public and private companies and their records on environment, employee training programs, diversity programs, safety and quality, profit sharing, tuition assistance, military contracts, women and minority advancement and work- and family-friendly policies.

You might even pick up something from a company's mission statement.

In general, don't ask questions that would put someone on the defensive. Marty told me about an interview she had, which was going well until the end. The employer asked, "Do you have any questions?" Marty, who worked in the same industry the company was in, said, "I noticed your company is not in the circle of people I know. You don't seem to network much. Is that something you want to change?"

She found out later that question nixed her from the job offer. The interviewer saw it as a criticism.

It Can Wait

Later down the line you can ask to see the employee handbook and review policies such as family leave and sick leave. But wait until you know the company is really interested in you.

This will also be the time to check out things that can cause you stress on the job. For example, if it's an issue with you, find out if there's smoking in the office. I had one client who was job-hunting because he couldn't stand to be around the smokers at the company. Other things that cause stress are noise, overtime, travel, deadlines, temperature, chemicals or materials you come in contact with and office space. As you get more serious about the position, ask to take a tour of the offices so you can see if it's conducive to you.

Smart companies will give you the chance to talk to employees to get a feel for attitudes and company culture. If they don't, ask if you can talk to people who work there—again, wait until you know the company is interested in you.

THINGS TO TATTOO ON YOUR BRAIN

If you're going to present yourself in the best possible light, you'll need to tell an employer:

- About your strengths and knowledge
- The reason you're looking for a job
- Where you've been and where you want to go

. . . and articulate all of that in a positive way, with the right interview attitude and knowing it like the back of your hand.

No problem? Diana is a bright and articulate professional who came to me after she left her last position. She was applying for a job in the financial services industry.

When I asked her about her *strengths and expertise*, she said: "My people skills, technical skills and overall framework of the financial problem-solving models."

Huh?

When I asked her *why she was looking for a job*, she said: "I invested much time into developing strategic plans for our company. The plans fell on deaf ears. I was tired of their apathy. The management philosophy was ineffective and the company was going downhill fast. When my husband got an opportunity to move to San Diego, I decided this was a great time to leave."

When I asked about her *career objective*, she said: "I've had positions of increasing responsibility in the financial services industry and demonstrated successful leadership, and want to find a company that will challenge and enhance my experience and skills."

But what does she want to do?

You may not think her responses were so bad. But an employer hears answers that:

- Are vague and unclear
- Don't answer the questions
- Describe what she didn't like
- Reek of negativity
- Don't explain what she does
- Display a "what can you do for me" attitude

Diana is typical. From the least experienced to the most seasoned, most people have never really thought about these basic questions. So their answers lack strategy and foresight. Don't wing it. This information must be thought out, planned and practiced.

A Four-step Exercise to Explain the Basics

1. Get clear on what your strengths are.

These are the skills you enjoy using most and that come most naturally. You determined those in chapter one.

2. Write out everything you know about.

This is listed under your expertise, which you defined in chapter one. You will use this information to create a statement that summarizes your body of knowledge and experience. This may seem elementary, because *you* know what you know. The interviewer doesn't.

Now you're ready to write your *Personal Overview*. This gives both your strengths and an overview of your expertise and experience. Then we'll move on to steps three and four.

EXAMPLE OF PERSONAL OVERVIEW

I have eighteen years of experience in production, packaging and materials management in the pharmaceutical and health care industries, with specific expertise in project management, budgeting, distribution and transportation management and inventory control. I have the knowledge and experience to oversee a manufacturing and distribution operation and I enjoy managing, leading teams and giving presentations. I also speak Japanese and have worked extensively overseas in the Japanese market.

3. Develop a rationale for why you're job hunting.

Write down the facts of why you are looking: You were let go; The company downsized and eliminated your job; Your company went bankrupt; You left by choice; You moved. In other words, why are you in this situation today?

Now, no offense, but I bet, you just listed more than the facts. Some little comment slipped in there. Go back and look for opinions, judgments and fingerpointing in what you just wrote, such as: The

company management was stupid; I was tired of the lack of accountability in the organization's ranks; My boss was a jerk; Management lied; The management philosophy was ineffective; My boss knew less than I did and was intimidated; I was the only one without a college degree; I was paid more than anyone else.

Even if you believe that's what happened, don't say it. It's explosive language, and it will banish you from the interview process faster than you can say, "But I didn't mean anything bad . . ." Rewrite the reason you were let go *without* editorial comment.

Show this to someone who can be objective. Ask him: "How does this hit you?" If he says, "OK," take the paper out of his hand and ask, "Why am I looking for a job?" If he says "Because your company didn't care about you," your editorial comment still comes through. Ask him, "Why do you say that?" Probe him until he can't point out anything that sounds negative.

EXAMPLE OF A RATIONALE FOR SOMEONE WHOSE JOB WAS ELIMINATED

I worked for The Adele Company for the past ten years, starting as a sales trainee and progressively moving up to Director of Sales and Marketing. I enjoyed my work there and had a very responsible position. The company was recently bought by a foreign investor and, as a result, my entire department was eliminated. I'm obviously disappointed about this, but I am looking forward to contributing my experience and skills to another firm.

4. Create your objective—a statement that describes what you want to move toward and how you will contribute.

Most people can do the opposite: Describe what they want to get away from and how the company can help them.

OK, now that you've written your *Personal Overview* and you can articulate your strengths and expertise, the first part of your objective will be easy. (I'll show you how that fits in in a minute.) The second part of your objective includes how you will make a difference. These are phrases that tell how you affect the bottom line.

EXAMPLES OF HOW YOU CAN MAKE A DIFFERENCE

- Contribute to a company's ability to achieve and maintain government compliance.
- Enhance the positive image of an organization.
- Contribute to the efficiency and smooth operations of a health care organization.
- Promote the value of a company's products or services.
- Increase sales.
- Develop customized software to enhance quality control.
- Ensure maximum equipment productivity.
- Ensure the distribution of freight and deliveries.
- Contribute to increased market growth.
- Implement modern technology and manufacturing processes to maintain a competitive edge.
- Enhance the quality and performance of a company's product.
- Design equipment that results in cost-effective systems.
- Maximize the potential of human resources.
- Create positive and lasting customer relationships.

Add to that your strengths and expertise, and you've got your objective.

EXAMPLE OBJECTIVE

I'm looking for a position where I can contribute to a food manufacturer's ability to achieve and maintain international market competitiveness. I want to use my strong skills in building and managing a staff and giving effective presentations, and to apply my strengths and knowledge in strategic and international marketing and background in manufacturing.

All of this—your strengths, expertise, reason for job hunting and objective—must be tattooed on your brain before you go to a job interview.

So if I asked Diana the same three questions I listed earlier in this chapter:

1. What are your strengths and expertise?
2. Why are you looking for a job?
3. What's your career objective?

. . . here is a much better response:

Personal Overview (Strengths and Expertise)

My background encompasses fourteen years in financial services, in which I moved from management trainee to vice president of our regional branches. My expertise includes hands-on experience with mergers, acquisitions and training. I have a thorough understanding of all financial products and am very skilled in explaining in simple terms what they are, their benefits and how to sell them to a diverse market. I enjoy training, leading teams and giving presentations to staff and management.

Reason for Job Hunting

I had intended to stay with Sixth National Bank. I enjoyed the work and the people. I was instrumental in helping the organization become the second-largest bank in this area. However, I am from San Diego, my family is all here, and we've decided we want to be closer to them. So I am committed to being here.

Career Objective

Now I am exploring the financial services industry to find an organization that can use my knowledge and experience to increase its market growth in an extremely competitive time. In particular, I would like to play an instrumental part in recruiting and building a well-trained and knowledgeable staff that can sell a multitude of financial products.

In chapter seven you'll see how this well-thought-out career objective enhances your communication skills.

SUMMARY

You need to do five things to put yourself in a position of strength before you even walk through the company's doors (see the checklist). But don't do any of this to impress the interviewer. Do it for the only two reasons that will help you get The Job You Want:

- To present yourself as a mature, professional problem solver
- To have information that will help you know

whether the company and position are the right ones for you

CHECKLIST
- ✔ Find out what the company does, who runs it, a brief history and the financial status.
- ✔ Know the pay range for the position and where you fit in.
- ✔ Coach and follow up with your references.
- ✔ Prepare answers and questions that reflect a "what can I do for you" attitude.
- ✔ Know your strengths, expertise, reason for job hunting and objective like the back of your hand.

CHAPTER 5

You're Not Behind the Wheel, So . . .

Strategy #5

Be prepared for anything.

You're in the door—or you will be, anyway. Expect the company to study each step you take—literally and figuratively. And as long as you want to explore a relationship with them, your goal is to present each step you take in the best possible light.

Obviously, they can't really know you in one interview. But they will still judge you. They'll look at every minute detail of how you talk, gesture, stand and, for the purpose of this chapter, how well you handle anything they throw at you.

They're in the driver's seat at this point. I've never heard of a company asking a candidate how he or she would like to be interviewed. So the company will set the agenda. It helps if you're prepared for anything.

Don't be surprised if you take a round of personality and aptitude tests for an entire morning, go to lunch with three managers, take a tour, meet with five new people in the afternoon and give a presentation—all in one day and for one job.

Let's go through potential situations and interview techniques you could face and how to handle them. The responses I suggest should not necessarily be used verbatim. I give them to demonstrate the attitude you want to convey and the point you're trying to establish. Weigh your particular situation and use the responses I've provided as guidelines.

INTERVIEW TECHNIQUES

You can run into a variety of interview styles and techniques. Most interviewers will ask predetermined questions, as well as go along with the flow of the conversation.

I don't list these techniques to scare you. And I don't want to lead you to believe that all interviewers are out to trip you up. Just be aware that there are various techniques and styles. You can tell a lot about the individual and even the company by the way you are interviewed.

Psyching You Out: Behavioral Interviews

Interviewers often use this technique when they want insight into how you will handle a situation or problem. It helps them understand how you've acted in the past, and enables them to draw conclusions about how you will react in the future. They do this by asking how you handled a specific event.

- What did you do when that client you told me about changed the copy five minutes before it was going to the printer?
- What about the time that customer started swearing at you?
- Was that the right thing to do?
- What did you do when that employee started crying?
- What was the most difficult business problem you encountered and what did you do?
- Tell me about a time when you were under tremendous pressure and how you handled it.
- Tell about a time you didn't get what you wanted with a customer, co-worker, manager or classmate.

Questions that start off with "Tell me about a time you did such and such . . ." are behavioral questions.

Tip:

• Stay on your toes. If you get into specifics, explain the situation and how you resolved it. (I tell how to do this in chapter seven.)

You might also hear questions that are based on hypothetical situations:

• What would you do if a major project you were working on wasn't going to meet the deadline?
• What would you do if an employee became violent?
• How would you fire someone?
• What would you do if I came to you at five o'clock and asked you to finish a project by morning, but you had a six o'clock commitment?
• What would you do if you were forced to work with someone you didn't get along with on a project only the two of you could handle?

Tip:

• Think through what the interviewers want to know and address it. For example, if you were asked the question about not meeting the deadline of the major project, what do you think they're fishing for?

First of all, it probably happens a lot or has been a problem before. The interviewers may want to see:

• How you would handle it
• What strategy you would use
• How you'd cope
• If you would negotiate
• How resourceful you are
• If you would think to add personnel
• If you could cut corners without compromising the project

Tip:

• You may not be able to answer a question without more information. It's fine to say that how you'd react would depend on the exact circumstances. Then you can give an example of a similar situation

that did happen. Just be sure to also explain how well you handled it. If possible, end your story with the results of how this made the situation or company better.

You might hear questions about how you will solve a problem you'll be expected to handle:

• What will you do to increase sales in this district?
• How will you lead the company to stay competitive?
• How will you improve our customer service?
• How will you develop better relationships with the press?

Tip:

• It may not be as easy as pie, so don't be too quick to give an answer. You don't know enough about the problem, the company and the people yet. Say that.

"This is obviously a complex issue. So I would need more information about the daily operations before I could give you a valid answer. And I would want to talk to the staff to hear what they think the problems are, to get them to buy into the process and to become involved in the solution. That's the only way we could solve it. Having said that, I can, though, give you an example of how I improved customer service in my last position."

This answer tells the interviewer you understand the issues involved, gives insight into your approach, demonstrates maturity and leadership and ends with an example of your potential based on your past.

Getting Your Goat: Stress-producing Interviews

The heat gets turned up when you run into these type of interviews. You could encounter one when interviewers want to see how well you handle pressure. You're in a stress-producing interview when they fire a series of difficult questions in a gruff manner.

If you've ever watched a court trial, you've seen this approach in action. In a rapid-fire series of questions, an attorney attacks one of the defense witnesses with something like: "You have no specific forensic training, isn't that correct? . . . You've never taken a class in forensic science? . . . You've never taught a class in forensic science? . . . You have no training whatsoever in police evidence-gathering techniques, correct?"

These are the kinds of questions people have heard in an interview:

- Why in the world would you want to work for us when you've had your own business all these years?
- Why would you go to work for a small company like ours when you've been with a Fortune 500 company, made a good salary with great perks and had a company car?
- Tell me exactly how you conducted that review.
- Why did you take that job when it had nothing to do with your education?
- I heard you got fired from your last job.

One woman's day of interviews for an organizational development position at a West Coast company started off with an interviewer who seemed to be using this technique. She describes how uncomfortable it was.

"The interviewer seemed almost hostile. She just began firing questions. She was extremely intense and wanted to hear details. This seemed odd for such a short interview and I found myself in a defensive mode. It almost felt like she was putting me through drills. At the end, she lightened up."

Remember, interviewers use this technique to see if you become upset, defensive, even hostile under pressure. If it truly is a stress interview, it's not done to be nasty. They're trying to catch you off guard. Don't let them get your goat. Show the interviewer how well you handle stress by staying calm and answering the questions as best as you can.

Stress interviews are not that common, and you may not encounter one unless you're interviewing for a high-stress position.

Tip:

- If you feel the questions are coming too fast and you're not answering them effectively, don't hesitate to take a deep breath and, with a smile, say "Could I take one question at a time? I think I could give you a better answer that way."

This type of treatment can influence your feelings about the company. In the case of the woman I just talked about, only one out of eight people conducted that type of interview. So don't make hasty judgments.

Marcy was a client of mine who was interviewing for a position at a health care facility. She described her interview with the president of the company: "He tried to rattle me from the beginning until I left. It was almost like an episode on the TV program *Columbo*. I'm literally walking out the door and he says, 'You know there will be a drug test.' I turned around and replied, 'That's no problem.' He just continued to throw things at me to see how I'd react."

In this case, this man's behavior and other clues she picked up did affect how she felt about working for the company. When she was offered the position, she turned it down.

Taking the Words out of Your Mouth: Interviews Over a Meal

These take place when:

- You're being seriously considered for the job and the company wants to get to know you in a less formal environment, to observe your social graces and how you treat strangers. (Use this opportunity to check them out, as well.)
- The job requires entertaining and they want to see how well you do in an out-of-the-office setting.
- They want to meet your spouse because (a) he or she may be meeting clients when you entertain, or (b) they're trying to woo you and want your spouse to feel comfortable.
- The interview is being held in another city or it's an all-day affair.

Tips:

- Don't go famished. You still need to concentrate on the main reason you're there—your presentation and getting information.
- Order food that's easy to eat.
- Brush up on your table manners.
- Don't drink alcoholic beverages.

A manager once wrote to me about an employee who was transferring to his division. He knew the person and was comfortable with his technical expertise, but he was concerned about his lack of social graces. The employee would be dealing with customers a lot in social settings. Since the manager knew him, he was willing to work with the man. But a new employer may not be as understanding.

If you don't know proper dining etiquette, take a class. Courses are usually offered by etiquette consultants. Look them up in the yellow pages of your phone book. They'll cover everything from the cocktail hour conversation to the right way to eat soup.

Even then, you never know what to expect. One job hunter interviewing for a senior executive position told me about the night the company invited him to a fancy restaurant for dinner.

"We sat in the private dining room—ten other company executives and I. After dinner, the waiter brought the check, and one by one they left the room. Finally, all of them were gone. I sat there for awhile waiting for someone to come back. No one did. I wondered if this was some kind of joke or mistake. I didn't know what to do. I went out and talked to the manager, who said they had all left. So I told the waiter there must have been some kind of misunderstanding, but that I would take care of the bill."

He later found out the company had arranged this scenario with the waiter in advance. They were trying to see how poised and calm he would be in a stressful situation and how graciously he would represent the company. By the way, they did reimburse him. Usually the employer foots the bill. If it's just you and one or two others, you can always offer to pay or go Dutch.

Put on Your Traveling Shoes: Interviews Out of Town

I think these can be the most stressful because you have to contend with getting there, meeting over meals, talking with many different people and dealing with accommodations if you stay overnight. Many times you don't have a moment to yourself because someone picks you up at the airport and takes you to breakfast, lunch and dinner.

Once I had an interview with a firm in Pennsylvania. My plane left at 7:30 A.M. and arrived in a major snowstorm. The flight was delayed and I was two hours late for our meeting. By then it was noon, so the president and I went straight to lunch. I barely had a chance to establish rapport with her.

We were walking down the cobblestone sidewalk in blinding sleet. I was wearing a flimsy raincoat and heels; she had the umbrella. My shoe got caught in a brick and she didn't notice. She just continued walking, talking about what a lovely town this was. I called out, but she didn't hear me. I did catch up with her. It was a disastrous interview.

If you have an interview out of town, be prepared to take tests, meet with various people and have meetings over meals. This may be their only shot at checking you out, so they will want to cram in as much as possible. Get plenty of sleep the night before. You might be traveling to a different time zone and could have a very stressful day ahead.

Amy describes the interview she had out of town as a "total brain drain." It included eight hours of tests to complete *before* she arrived. "Once there, they gave me another four hours of timed tests on personality and aptitude. I had interviews, gave a presentation and received three hours of feedback from them on the tests I took. Because I am in human resources, one of my tests was to take the results of someone else's tests and give them written and verbal feedback."

Tips:

Do as much as you can up front to feel confident and poised during the interview:

• Double check that you have packed everything you need. (Women should take two pairs of hose; men should take two ties.)

• Don't check your luggage if the flight is not direct; your clothes may not arrive when you do.

• Take an alternate outfit. Once, I was giving a presentation in Minneapolis. That morning I hung my suit in the shower of my hotel room to get out the wrinkles. While I was running the hot water to create steam, the entire suit fell in the tub and was drenched.

Around the World: Interviews in Other Countries

Every country and culture has its own customs and, therefore, interview etiquette. If you're interviewing in a foreign country and with a native of that country, find out the specific customs or peculiarities when it comes to nonverbal and verbal communications. Research the culture and proper behavior on everything from dress, to social etiquette and table manners.

Be prepared for interview questions that you would consider inappropriate if you heard them in this country. Here, we focus on asking questions that relate to your professional qualifications. Outside the United States, some employers will put more emphasis on your personal life: They might ask about your family life, age, marital status, how much you socialize, what social and political organizations you belong to or how much you drink.

I'm telling you this so you don't walk out in a huff. Hopefully, you'll be prepared by understanding that this is a cultural difference, and you'll demonstrate your sensitivity in the way you answer the question.

On the other hand, even in a foreign country, some interviewers will ask the kinds of questions you'd hear in an interview in the United States.

Let's See How Much We Can Cram Into One Day: All-day Interviews

These take place most often—but not always—when the company brings you in town for an interview. They can start early in the morning and can include a variety of techniques and interviewers. Laura's all-day-interview experience for a job as a trainer at an international manufacturer went like this:

"They flew me in on Sunday. I found a packet at my hotel room that explained the next day's schedule, information on a tour of the company I could take, bios of the interview team and articles on the company. I took the company tour, and the next morning arrived at their offices at 7:40. They put me in a small room and six different people came to me throughout the day. Each interview was an hour. They used an interview methodology that asked specific questions to determine if I had the characteristics to be successful in the job.

"First, each person asked a few of the same questions. Then, each one had a particular focus. I got tired of answering the same questions over and over. They gave me an hour break after the first interview. It was stressful, because after the first hour I was really pumped, and then they stopped.

"By the time I got to the second interview, I had to get pumped up again. Then there were two hours straight of interviewing, lunch with someone, then two more hours straight and another hour break. At four, I was ready to scream 'Get me out of here!' By 5:10 I was in a cab to the airport. They also had given me a list of problem-solving exercises I might face on the job, which they wanted me to complete and mail back."

Barbara's experience at a company in Seattle included a variety of interviewers and styles. "Their recruiting van picked me up to go to my interviews. They actually have two people whose full-time jobs are to shuttle people around to interviews. I met with the hiring manager in the department I'd work in. He spent most of our time giving me an orientation to the division. Lunch was with four people I had already met and one new manager. I could hardly eat because they asked me so many questions about how I would handle specific situations.

"Back at the company, I met with a manager who was introverted, had no eye contact and asked more specific questions, such as 'How would you do a needs analysis?' He took copious notes and at the end I felt like I wanted to ask him if I passed the test. He was hard to read. After a very conversational meeting with another seven managers, I had dinner with six people, one of whom had just completed his first day on the job. It was more social than anything."

Tips:
- Get plenty of sleep the night before.
- It's easy to peter out after answering the same question over and over. Don't let your weariness or frustration show. Remember, the next person you meet with didn't hear what you just told the last one.
- Don't let your hair down, even in a more social situation.

It Takes Two . . . or Three: More Than One Interviewer

You could find yourself in an interview with not one, but two or three people. This saves the company time and gives everyone the same information to evaluate. These interviews can also be stressful.

Tips:
- When introduced, shake everyone's hand. Get a business card at the end; you will be writing everyone a thank-you note.

• Some people in the group will seem friendlier than others. To boost your confidence at the beginning, find the people (or person) who seem the most receptive and direct comments to them, still acknowledging the others. I find myself doing that when I give presentations to groups. I look for the people who nod, smile and give me feedback. It helps me connect at first.

• Also find the tough nuts in the crowd and win the confidence of the people who aren't so supportive. One of my clients was going to his third interview with a company. He had no experience, but the president liked him and wanted to hire him. My client, Jeff, had to have the blessing of the president's partner, a real tough cookie, before he could be hired.

When the partner met Jeff, she didn't offer to shake his hand and acted as if she didn't want to waste her time talking to him. She didn't think they should hire someone so inexperienced.

He told me, "I knew I was on trial. So I stared at her, letting her know 'I know you're unconvinced.' But I had gone through three interviews and was determined not to lose it on this one. I looked her in the eye and said, 'Let 'er rip.' She looked at her partner and seemed to relax a bit. I got the job."

In most circumstances, I wouldn't have recommended he say that. But he was there—I wasn't—and after sizing up the situation, he decided it was the best way to handle it. It worked.

• Scope out the group for the people who carry the most weight and may influence the hiring decision. Make sure you get a good read on them. Do they look convinced, confused or what? Address their concerns.

• Other times you interview with more than one person, but at different times. Each one may ask completely different questions than the last one. If asked the same questions over and over, as Laura was in her interviews, patiently answer them again and again.

Does Everyone Agree?
Interviews by Committee

Nonprofit organizations and universities can have "search committees" that screen and interview applicants. They are required to do this if they receive federal funding and must prove they are equal opportunity employers.

The committees are made up of at least one member of a minority and people with different philosophies and expertise to ensure that the interview process is not biased. To further ensure that, the committee will ask each applicant the same list of questions.

The committee either screens resumés as a group or each committee member brings his or her recommendations to the group. The goal is to choose the top five candidates.

One of my clients interviewed at a large nonprofit agency for a communications position. When she walked into the room where the interview was to take place, she was ushered to a chair surrounded by nine people in a semicircle. Each person took a turn asking questions.

In this situation as well, get everyone's business card. This will ensure that you have the correct spelling of names when you write thank-you notes— yes, even if there are nine of them.

Tips:

• Keep reminding yourself that they are only people. Even though they outnumber you, they are not there to intimidate you, but to get to know you. They want you to feel comfortable. They are trying to make this a fair process by meeting as a committee.

• Be pleasant, smile a lot and above all, just as you would in a one-on-one interview, be yourself.

Off the Beaten Track:
Interviews in Odd Places

Hotel rooms. They can be weird if there is a bed in the room. Hopefully, the interviewer, if he is going to rent a hotel room for the purpose of interviewing, will get one that has an adjoining room with only a desk, chairs and a couch. Usually, the interviewer will tell you what room to go to, or to ask for a specific name or company at the front desk.

Tip:

• Be sure to knock before you enter the room. There may be another interview in progress.

Hotel lobbies. These are difficult because strangers keep walking by catching snippets of your conversation. And it's easy to be distracted because of all the activity around you.

Tip:
• Try to find a table in a corner away from the traffic.

This Is a Test: Interview by Assessment Center

This is a "job simulation" test. The words "assessment center" describe the structure in which the tests are presented. It is an extremely useful way for companies to predict your future behavior or performance based on how you act during one of these tests.

The techniques are used most often when interviewing key decision-makers in organizations or for positions that require a lot of administrative tasks, deal with many supervisors or involve facing emergency situations. This can get costly for an employer, but gives them a lot of insight into you. In the long run, hiring the right person can save a company money.

Here's how it might work. You are put in a group made up of the other candidates being considered for the job. For anywhere from two to three days, you go through exercises that some psychologist thought up that are supposed to reveal how you handle situations you could face in the job.

For example, your group is given a problem: "There has been a security leak in the company regarding the ingredients of our new, hot product. Solve it."

Or the interviewer actually sets the stage for a real-life, day-to-day circumstance you would encounter. For example, if you are interviewing for the position of city manager, the interviewer might set up a mock city council meeting. Real-life council members would ask you questions about how you would respond to or deal with problems.

You could also be set up to face a real-life emergency issue. For example, if you were interviewing for a key decision-making role, such as president of an organization, or one that deals with the public, you might be thrown this dilemma: "There's just been a shooting in your company. The media (possibly real-life members) are waiting for you outside your office. What are you going to do?"

Now, there's a well-trained panel of observers, either in the room or behind glass, assessing and rating your ability to receive, translate and respond to problems. The panel might include the human resource director of the organization that's doing the hiring, a recruiter, employees of the organization who have knowledge of the position, and even the company psychologist. They have a list of skills you will need to succeed in this job. They rate you accordingly.

The observers watch to see—in a group situation—who takes the lead, how effectively you lead or facilitate a group, your personal impact on the group and your skills in relating to others. They also look at how you respond to critical and everyday situations and if you have the experience, temperament and skills to deal with the issues you'll face on the job.

You might also be given a written exercise. They call these "in-basket" tests because you are presented with letters, stacks of memos or reports you'd find in your in-basket at the job and you're asked to act on them. They're looking for:

• How you prioritize
• How you handle issues or problems
• How you spot problems

They could also ask you to address a specific issue. For instance: Write a one-page news release regarding the shooting in your company. Or: Here's a project you would be working on in this position. You've got two hours to do it. Write down what you'd do.

By the way, you can get feedback on your performance. People who have gone through them usually say good things about the experience. They can be very valuable for you to see your strengths or areas that need improvement.

Here's another assessment technique a recruiter told me he uses to evaluate someone for a position that must handle emergencies and demonstrate composure, alertness and the ability to stand up for himself:

"I will make something on their chair unstable, so it's safe to sit on but it doesn't sit right and is noticeable to the candidate. Whether a person says something about it or not tells you whether he speaks up for himself.

"I will also call a potential police or fire chief in the middle of the night to see how he answers the phone—whether he's calm, angry or alert."

HOW TO PREPARE:

- Write down the kinds of daily problems and issues you could encounter on the job.
- Write down the kinds of emergency situations you might face.
- Think through the skills you will need to succeed on a daily basis and in emergency situations. How would you react? How have you handled similar situations in the past? Why were you successful?

Interviews With People Who Are Terrible Interviewers

People tell me all the time how badly an interview went because the person conducting it was ill-prepared or ineffective. It's true, some people are great managers, accountants, geologists or teachers but don't know diddly about conducting job interviews.

Interviewers who work in personnel are usually more savvy. But anybody can be biased without realizing it. For example, people like to hire people who are like themselves. Other times, they make their decision about whether they want to hire you in the first four minutes after meeting you.

Bad interviewers can also include someone who:

- Only talks about the company or position and never gives you a chance to talk
- Doesn't ask questions to give you the opportunity to share relevant information
- Is unfocused
- Keeps interrupting your meeting to take phone calls or talk to someone

Some of these situations can be remedied, or you may at least be able to have some influence, if you watch for your opportunities.

Tips:

- If he does all the talking, look for *subtle* ways to influence the direction of the conversation.

If the interviewer says: "The person in this position must be able to handle customer relations, especially issues that come up regarding billing," before he goes on say something like: "That's an area I'm quite experienced in. In fact, in my last position, I managed a ten-person department that did nothing but deal with customer billing."

At the same time, keep in mind that when someone talks a lot, he usually likes you. It can indicate that he is comfortable with you. Although this can be a good sign, you still want to watch for opportunities to share without interrupting or breaking the natural flow of the conversation.

- If she doesn't ask questions, wait until she shares specific requirements for the job, and ask: "Would you like to hear how I've done something like that in my present job?"
- If she's unfocused, which inhibits you from getting or giving information, ask questions before she moves on to another point by saying: "Before you move on, could you tell me more about the responsibilities of the position?"
- If the interview continues to be interrupted by phone calls or people walking in with emergencies, you may just have to go with the flow. It depends on the interviewer's personality and style. If he seems flexible or keeps apologizing, this may be your clue to say something like: "Mr. Mechel, I can see that you have some unexpected issues coming up this morning. Perhaps this just isn't a good time. Would you like to reschedule our interview?"

Mr. Mechel will either realize he's doing you both an injustice and ask that he not be interrupted, or he will apologize and most likely appreciate your offer.

Sometimes you can't do much at the time. One of my clients, who is a financial manager, was interviewing with a large company that hired an outside consultant to conduct the interviews. The consultant actually fell asleep while my client was talking. In that case, I think my client had a right—and a duty to the company—to tell them about this man's conduct.

IS IT A GOOD MATCH? YOU CAN FEEL IT IN YOUR BONES
The Guy Would Be a Jerk to Work for

One of the worst interviews I ever experienced was with the president of an advertising agency who not only took phone calls and read his mail during our meeting, but sat with his feet propped up on his desk and smoked a cigar. It was his office, so he could do whatever he wanted. I sat politely through our meeting, but had no interest in working for someone who treated people so rudely.

Another time I was sitting in the lobby of a training company waiting for the president to return to his office for our first interview. We had never met, so neither of us knew what the other one looked like. I was alone in this very small lobby when a man walked in the front door, whisked past me and bumped my leg without any acknowledgment. I remember thinking, "I hope that's not him." It was. That incident, too, told me a lot about the person I would be reporting directly to.

Sarah, a health care professional, shared this story with me: "I made up my mind that I wouldn't feel comfortable working for this man when we talked on the telephone. He talked to me on his speaker phone the entire time. How rude. How lazy."

I Couldn't Picture Myself There

Tony's feelings about a company's physical surroundings made him question his comfort level in working there. "The place was old and the security was intense. I had to sign in and out every time I went into a different department, giving my name and address and country of origin. The employee who accompanied me had to sign in with his employee number. There were metal detectors. I just couldn't see myself in that environment."

Our Priorities Don't Match

Barbara's interview at a consulting firm and subsequent rejection for the position left her feeling insecure.

"They asked me questions that I wasn't prepared for—test questions about the company I work for now. For instance, 'What's the best-selling product your company has overseas?' This is not the kind of information I would deal with in my job. Plus, I had been busy researching *their* company.

"One of the men asked me if I thought a particular company would ever get on the Internet. I responded by saying something about it seeming unlikely due to the security issue. I hadn't read the day's newspaper, and when I got back to my hotel that afternoon, I saw the paper. There was an article about the fact that the company he had asked me about had joined the Internet that day! They were so into details. I'm a big-picture person."

Barbara may have learned what kinds of things to be prepared to answer. But she may also con-

clude that she does not fit in with what they want—people who are so concerned with details. And how about the way they tried to see how current she was on a particular news item? Their approach feels almost dishonest.

Julie, a nursing home administrator, felt uncomfortable about what she noticed as she toured a facility with the director.

"The place was well cared for and had a good reputation, but as we walked through the halls he didn't say hello to the residents. The people just didn't seem to be a priority to him. Also, based on the things he said, he seemed to view the place solely as a business. He was only concerned about the bottom line. I began to envision a time that I would go to him to say 'I think we should do such and such for better quality,' and he'd immediately respond with 'How's that affect the bottom line?' Our priorities didn't match."

Our Values Don't Match

Another job hunter told me about an interviewer who made some odd inquiries.

"He kept poking around for something I couldn't quite put my finger on. He asked what five values my parents had taught me. . . . What were my other influences as I was growing up. He asked questions that bordered on the personal. He didn't seem to care about my skills and experience. I later found out that this man has staunch religious beliefs and prefers to hire people who believe as he does. He seemed judgmental and rigid, and I could just tell it wasn't a place for me."

We've Got Similar Styles and Expectations

"I knew this company was a good match because of the professionalism they exhibited in their work and the way they treated me," Marilyn told me after she accepted a position. "I'm a very organized person and like things clearly defined. They had these big charts that designated their sales, products and people working on projects across the country.

"The goals and expectations of the job were clearly laid out. They told me where the job would lead. They invest a lot of training in their people. I was really impressed when, at the end of our meeting, the vice president said, 'If you think this is a good match, you call me at the end of the week. We think it's positive, but we want you to feel comfortable.' "

Chris flew to Texas for an interview with a very young and progressive computer manufacturer. "The company flew both my husband and me down on Thursday for my first interview. Friday morning, a driver named James picked me up in a white Lincoln.

"The first interviewer asked me to tell her about a project I felt good about, something I didn't feel good about and what I had learned. I learned a lot about the company by the way they interviewed me. It was pretty loosey-goosey compared to other companies. Only one woman had a list of typed questions that she asked and filled in the answers. I also met with a peer. His role was to answer my questions and give me a tour of the plant.

"They were pretty laid back. At my company, everything would have been so structured and programmed, I wouldn't have sat around for a second. We stayed for the weekend, which I thought was very generous of the company. It gave us a chance to explore the area and see how we liked it."

They're Flexible and Sensitive to Family Needs

At Barbara's interview at a West Coast software developer, the second manager she met with was late because the manager had just gotten a call from her nanny. Apparently, the nanny had a contagious disease and couldn't be around the manager's son.

"So I hopped into the car with the manager, went to her home, picked up her eighteen-month-old boy and brought him back to the office. She interviewed me in the car and at her house. She kept asking me to forgive her for not maintaining eye contact while she was driving. I enjoyed that interview. It was real life. And it told me a lot about the company and how comfortable she felt about bringing her son to the office."

CHECKLIST

You'll be your most effective when you are prepared to:

✔ Present yourself and your qualifications many times to several people or to a committee, in the office or over a meal.

✔ Stay on guard but calm and poised if an interviewer throws you a curve to see how you handle pressure or conflict.

✔ Anticipate the kinds of issues and problems you would address in this position. (Be prepared to explain how you handle problems by giving examples of similar situations you successfully faced in the past.)

✔ Look for ways to influence and direct the conversation if you haven't had a chance to share relevant information.

CHAPTER 6

When Words Get in the Way

Strategy #6

Spot-check language, attitudes and topics that could sink you.

This strategy is for those how-do-you-not-say-your-boss-is-a-jerk-when-he-is, how-do-you-not-say-you-hate-your-company-when-you-do and what-do-you-do-if-you-don't-have-a-college-degree moments.

Those circumstances might all be true. But if you give one shred of evidence about how you feel or leak out one teensy-weensy drop of frustration, you're dead meat.

I never said interviewing was fair. That's why, in this chapter, you'll learn how to spot those killer words and phrases before they spill out. You'll see why it's so important to handle these and other circumstances with diplomacy and well-thought-out responses. That's why you need a strategy.

Certain language, attitudes and topics can prejudice interviewers in a second. Even if you didn't mean to imply something negative, you'll see how an innocent comment here or a minor slip of the tongue there could blow your chances for the job of your dreams.

I have organized this information into five parts:

1. Repositioning the way you see an interview
2. What not to talk about
3. What to do about perceived liabilities
4. How to overcome objections
5. Common communication blunders

LANGUAGE, ATTITUDES AND TOPICS
You're Not Selling Shoes: How to Reposition the Way You See an Interview

Think back to something I said in the Introduction. Remember I urged you to reposition how you

look at the job interview? Instead of seeing it as a performance where you must deliver your lines with perfection and persuade your audience to buy you, see it as an opportunity to present yourself in the best possible light while you explore if the job is a good fit.

This repositioning helps you relax and hold a conversation instead of a sales pitch. The traditional definition of "selling" would have you concentrate on trying to persuade someone to do something your way or to change his viewpoint.

You and the interviewer will get more out of your meeting if, instead, you concentrate on having an intelligent conversation to explore your potential union. You'll also take the pressure to "sell yourself" off.

As you practice interview questions, before you say anything, ask yourself "Does the information I'm about to share and the way I'm saying it present me in the best possible light?"

Pretend your mother is there. What would she think?

Just Say No: What Not to Talk About

BOSSES

You may hear a question such as "How do you get along with your boss?" or "What do you think of your present (or last) boss?"

Beware of these pitfalls your answers could create:

1. If you describe a boss you liked who is nothing

like this *potential* boss, the interviewer could conclude the two of you are incompatible.

2. If you point out what you consider negative attributes that describe the person interviewing you, the interviewer could conclude the two of you are incompatible.

3. If you say something good *or* bad about present or former bosses, you come across as judgmental.

You can't win. "Then what the heck do I say?" you're mumbling. I'm getting there.

Keep your answer neutral with these kinds of phrases:

- The person I report to in my present position is the Vice President of Operations. He's very experienced in the retail business.

- He's taught me a lot about mass merchandising, customer service and marketing. Since he's in Washington, I only see him twice a month.

- We have a good working relationship.

What if you can't stand your boss? Why do you need to share that with the interviewer? It makes no difference, and talking about it will detract from presenting yourself in the best possible light.

Just address the question in the most neutral way and move on.

"Wait," I can hear you protesting. "It's important to share best and worst boss stories because it helps weed out a boss I wouldn't get along with anyway." If your interviewer is your potential boss, that's unlikely. You're more likely giving your interviewer information about you that helps her weed *you* out.

There are other ways to determine what kind of boss someone might be (which I talked about in chapter five): Pay attention to his interviewing style, questions he asks and how you're treated.

Also, look back at chapter one, where you wrote down "What makes me feel appreciated by management" and "Environment I feel comfortable in." Develop questions to ask your interviewer that will help you spot clues. For example:

- How do people on your staff know they're doing a good job?
- How do you like to lead people?
- What is your management philosophy?

- Do you encourage entrepreneurship?

One man told me, "My situation is different. My boss for the last fifteen years has been my father. He was domineering and controlling. An interviewer will understand that." Not necessarily. Avoid discussions about the faults and attributes of former and present bosses—related or not.

PEOPLE PROBLEMS

A very messy can of worms will spill out all over the interviewer's desk with comments such as "I can't stand people who . . ." or "I have problems dealing with creative types . . . accounting types . . . men . . . women."

It's OK to bring up examples in which you helped resolve a problem that *involved* other people. Just be careful you don't sound critical or as if you have difficulty getting along with them.

For example, if you are asked, "What was the biggest problem you dealt with in your last job?" and the problem had to do with other people, here's an answer that treads into the danger zone. (A more appropriate answer follows.)

DANGER ZONE

"When I was in the billing department, we had a woman who constantly griped. She was a rotten apple and affected everybody. She'd complain about her pay, our boss, the other employees, the work, the president of the company, the customers. Things sure weren't perfect, but I can't stand people who just sit around and complain all day. What a pain she was. I hated coming to work. I think part of the problem was she was overweight and had a bad marriage. Finally, one day, I suggested we have a group meeting, which eventually led to our suggestion box."

She comes across as critical and negative. She puts more emphasis on what was wrong and talks little about the positive outcome.

COMFORT ZONE

"When I was in the billing department, there was an employee who shared her dissatisfaction about her job on a regular basis. It began to affect the entire department's morale. I suggested that we have a meeting of all the people in our department during lunch, which we did. As a group, we discussed issues we felt required management's attention, came up with suggestions on how to deal with them and presented them to our supervisor. As a result, we now give regular input to management. We created a suggestion box for the entire company and the employee who was so negative has totally changed her attitude."

She comes across as a problem solver, leader and team player. She didn't dwell on the "people problem" part, but on the resolution. *How* she describes this situation makes a big difference.

One man, when asked "What did you like least about your last job?" replied, "Working with manipulative and unscrupulous people." Whoa! Trying to explain that one (yes, the interviewer asked what he meant) just dug him deeper and deeper in trouble.

YOUR TROUBLES

If you got your walking papers, the company is downsizing, it eliminated your job, you had a bad experience at your last (or present) job, or you're having a hard time finding a job, it's unfortunate. But the interview is not the place to talk about it. No tearing down or bad-mouthing companies or people or telling hard luck stories. Ever.

You may have every reason to be angry or frustrated. Tell your family and friends about it. Cry, yell, complain, grumble, lament, mourn: Experience whatever you need to in order to deal with your "ending."

Find a trusted advisor and say everything that comes to your mind—as crazy as it may seem. Safely express your feelings, anger and fears outside the interview. Just get it off your chest *before* you go into an interview or you'll sound like a whiner. Interviewers don't hire whiners.

What do you say so you don't sound like one when you think you got a raw deal? Let's say you were, like one of my clients, laid off after years with a company and you're enraged. The interviewer asks the logical question on her mind: "Why did you leave your job?" You begin to foam at the mouth. You may want to say what he said:

DANGER ZONE

"The company was totally mismanaged. For years, we tried to tell them where we were headed, but no one listened. Then the Japanese came in and bought us and they closed our division. They have no loyalty to us, even though we were loyal our whole career. I didn't even get offered a retirement package."

He comes across angry and critical, and possibly vindictive and bigoted.

COMFORT ZONE

"I was with Brentino's for twenty-two years and thoroughly enjoyed my work there. Unfortunately, the market changed drastically with all the cuts in the military, and our business suffered. The company went through a major restructuring when it was purchased and our division was closed."

He comes across as realistic and practical.

Whether you are still employed, whether you left your job by choice or not, think through your response to questions that could get you churning. Stick to facts. This is especially important if you're someone who has not interviewed much, for a long time—or ever.

If I Only Had a Brain: What to Do About Perceived Liabilities

Most everyone seems to have a "perceived liability." These are situations, dynamics or circumstances that, by choice or not, you face. Sometimes they are things you lack or wish were different. "If I only had a college degree . . ." "If I only had more experience . . ." This becomes your particular "perceived liability," which you believe will create a problem in getting The Job You Want. These are the facts:

- You don't have a college degree
- You are a minority
- You are pregnant
- You are an older worker—over forty
- You are young and inexperienced
- You are disabled
- You are a career changer
- You haven't worked outside the home in a year or more
- You were laid off or fired

If you're standing, you may want to sit down when you hear this: The only liability you have is going into an interview believing you *have* a liability.

If you just jumped back up and yelled, "What? How can you say that? I *am* disabled . . . pregnant . . . a minority . . . over forty . . . I was fired . . . want to change careers . . ."—relax.

I'm not disputing the *facts* of your situation; I am disputing the *assumption* that your situation may hold you back from getting The Job You Want, or that the employer will see you as flawed. That assumption is what turns into a "perceived liability," which leads to you feeling powerless—like a victim.

Let's walk through this issue.

1. Could it be that you are the only one who thinks this "liability" exists? Sure, that's possible.

A man who had just quit his job of seventeen years came to see me about his concern in finding a new job. The first thing he said was:

"What about the fact that I don't have a degree?"

"What about it?" I asked.

"Well, it's going to be an issue," he said.

"How do you know?"

"Well, won't it?"

"Why would it be?"

"Well, I don't know, I just figured it would be," he concluded.

Aha! There lies the possible problem. It hadn't been an issue in the first twenty years of his career, but now that he was uncertain about his future, he began to focus on his fears. Fear is faith that something won't work out. It's based on a possible reality, not certainty.

2. Could it be that an employer does think your circumstances make you undesirable? Sure, that's possible, too.

But wait a minute . . . how would you know? You won't, unless he brings it up. Unless you're a mind reader, you don't know for certain what the employer will think. So again, make sure you're not imposing your own fears on the situation.

Now I can hear you saying, "But I just *know* he'll think it's a problem, anybody would." OK, I know what you're getting at. Let's assume he does believe it's a problem, has a preconceived notion or realistic concern. What can you do?

On the one hand, odds are he won't mention it if his concern has to do with the following:

- You are a minority
- You are pregnant
- You are an older worker—over forty
- You are disabled

Most employers are smart enough not to mess with these because they can lead to potential claims of discrimination. On the other hand, he may not know your age or if you are pregnant unless you tell him.

If your circumstances are more evident and he doesn't say anything about it, there's not much you can do. If he believes your age or state of pregnancy are reasons not to hire you, you're not going to change his thinking. Why would you want to work for somebody like that, anyway?

If you are concerned because you don't have a degree or lack experience, the employer may indeed bring these issues up. And because you are a strategic job hunter, you will have anticipated concerns over your "perceived liability." (I'll talk more about that soon.)

Whether an employer expresses his concern or not is not the point here—that's a whole other issue. You can't change his mind, especially if you don't know what's *on* his mind. The only thing you can change is *your* belief.

If you believe that because of your particular situation you will have difficulty getting The Job You Want, you are worrying about and putting emphasis on what you *don't* have. This is the opposite of how you want to think if you're going to get what you want.

Your belief is the only thing that matters. That's what holds you back or moves you forward. If you think it's a problem, it will be. You'll worry about an employer bringing it up and demonstrate uneasiness and insecurity when she does. You may even sound defensive in your response.

If you don't believe it will inhibit you, it won't.

Hold on. I'm not saying you shouldn't be realistic here: Definitely be prepared to deal with it if it comes up.

Get smart. Before any interview, think about:

- What characteristics does the ideal candidate have?
- What is the interviewer afraid I won't have?
- How might the interviewer define my "type"? In other words, what preconceived notions will

she have about me based on my background or situation?

Have a confident answer to overcome any concern and help move the interview in the direction you want—concentrating on what you *do* have. (I talk about how to overcome objections in part four.) But you don't have to believe it's a problem.

People put more emphasis on trying to deal with the interviewer's belief than their own. It needs to be the other way around. For one, you'll be more convincing in trying to persuade an interviewer to the contrary if you don't buy into, or even entertain, a perceived liability. Second, you can't change someone else's belief, but you can change yours.

The form on page 53 can help you do that.

Most of the situations are ones you can't change. If you lack a degree or training, you could go back to school. And if you're a career changer, you could decide not to change careers.

But if you're over forty, young and inexperienced, disabled, haven't worked outside the home in a year or more, or were laid off or fired, you cannot change your situation. By and large, you're where you are today because of choices you have made. You're just who you are; these are your circumstances.

But . . . : How to Overcome Objections

"I'm concerned that you don't have enough experience in marketing."

"I'm afraid you'd be bored."

"You seem overqualified for this position."

"You don't have a degree."

"You've never worked in this field."

"You haven't worked in this field for ten years."

These are objections. They are really fears the employer has about your ability to do the job or fit with the company. How will you know about them? An interviewer could express his concerns in one of three ways:

- Not-so-subtly
- Subtly
- No comment (but you sense it)

Whether objections are overtly expressed, implied or sensed—or if you feel certain it will be an issue—you may be able to influence the interviewer's opinion. Let's go through your options. We'll look at how Brad handled the objections he faced when he was interviewing for a job as a career consultant after seventeen years as a college professor. The interviewer's concerns were:

1. Brad would have no understanding of business, having been in a university setting
2. Brad wouldn't be able to relate to some of their clients: blue-collar workers
3. Brad would be too theoretical and use language clients wouldn't understand

The interviewer came out and said: "I'm concerned that your lack of experience in dealing with blue-collar people, because you've been in a university environment, would be a hindrance."

Brad responded:

"I can see why those would be concerns. Perhaps it would help if I tell you a little bit more about myself and why I don't see them as hindering me in this position. Besides teaching at the university, I have worked closely with several Fortune 500 and medium- and small-size companies as a consultant. I have worked one-on-one with their employees and have given workshops on communication skills and diversity. So I'm very familiar with issues people face in all types of businesses. In addition, I have had a lot of interaction with many kinds of people, having played on a major league softball team for the last fifteen years."

How did he do that?

1. Before the interview Brad made a list of the qualities, experience and characteristics the ideal candidate would have.
2. Then he made a list of what the interviewer might be afraid he *wouldn't* have.
3. Finally, he made a list of the preconceived notions that the interviewer might have about him, based on his background.
4. He went in armed with this ammunition and pulled it out when he needed it.

Going through this exercise also helped Brad feel more confident about his potential perceived liabilities.

If the interviewer had been more subtle, he might have said: "You have always worked in white-collar environments, is that correct?" His question might

FILL IN THE BLANKS.

I. GET IT OUT ON THE TABLE.

1. I believe that my perceived liability of _____
   could hinder me in getting The Job I Want.

II. I GOTTA BE ME.

2. Is there anything I can do to change my situation or dynamic? (The fact that I am a minority, disabled, without a degree, fired from the job, etc.) _____

3. If yes, what is it? _____
   _____
   _____

4. Am I willing to do that? _____

III. I CREATED THIS MONSTER.

5. As a result of my belief, I feel (helpless, frustrated, hurt, etc.) _____

6. Do I want to feel this way? _____

7. Is it helping me get anywhere? _____

8. If I don't want to feel this way and it's not getting me anywhere, am I open to changing my belief? (If yes, go to part IV. If your answer is no, you're setting yourself up as a victim and you're not ready to go after what you really want.) _____

IV. WASH THAT THOUGHT RIGHT OUT OF YOUR HEAD.

9. I am (disappointed that I never got a degree, was fired from my job, don't have experience; or I cannot change the fact that I am a minority, disabled, pregnant) _____
   _____
   _____

I now choose to look at this situation as circumstances that I accept and that are unrelated to my ability to get The Job I Want.

Signed _____

Date _____

Now tear this page out of the book and paste it on your bathroom mirror.

imply his concern. If Brad's antennae are tuned in, he would hear it and could say:

"Mr. Newberry, does that concern you?" *or*

"Mr. Newberry, much of my experience has been in the university setting. But I also have a lot of experience as a consultant, working closely with workers in manufacturing environments and blue-collar positions. I have worked one-on-one with employees and have given workshops on communication skills and diversity. So I'm very familiar with issues people face in all types of environments. In addition, I have had interaction with many kinds of people, having played on a major league softball team for the last fifteen years."

If the interviewer did not bring it up, but Brad sensed it or just felt it would be a natural concern, he could say:

"Much of my experience has been in the university setting. But I also have a lot of experience as a consultant, working closely with workers in manufacturing environments and blue-collar positions. I have worked one-on-one with employees and have given workshops on communication skills and diversity. So I'm very familiar with issues people face in all types of environments. In addition, I have had interaction with many kinds of people, having played on a major league softball team for the last fifteen years."

or

"It occurred to me that it might be a concern of yours that most of my experience has not been in a traditional business setting, and that I may not have a grasp of the kinds of issues your clients face. I'd like to assure you that besides teaching, I am a communications consultant to all types of businesses—manufacturers as well as service companies—and have a broad understanding of their problems on the job."

DEALING WITH THE OBJECTION

Brad applied the following steps. Depending on what the objection is, you can do one of the following things (or a combination thereof):

A. I hear ya.

Acknowledge the concern. This probably would not be your first reaction. Most people immediately go into defense mode, saying: "Oh, but I do have lots of experience in marketing" or "I know I wouldn't be bored . . ." and so on. Your protests probably won't get you where you need to be.

If you want to pursue this position, you need to initiate a dialogue. The interviewer may have a concern because he doesn't have adequate information. (This was the case in Brad's situation.) He could have misunderstood something you said. You could have given a wrong impression. Or he could have a preconceived notion. (This also applied to Brad's situation.)

When you acknowledge his concern, you can almost hear a sigh of relief. This helps open that dialogue.

Say something like: "I can see why you might think that" or "I can understand your concern." Then you can either go to B (if you need or want more information) or move on to C.

B. Where are you coming from?

Ask "What makes you say that?" or "Could you tell me more about your concern?" This opens the way for him to tell you specifically how he has come to his conclusion.

In Brad's situation, the interviewer said "I'm concerned that your lack of experience in dealing with blue-collar people would be a hindrance."

Here's another example. Let's say you hear, "When you said you had never handled a press conference, I had grave concerns."

C. Let's clear this up.

Now that he told you his concern, or if you understand why he felt the way he did, you can correct this misunderstanding or fill in what he still needs to know by saying:

"I see. Mr. French, I didn't mean to give the impression that I had never handled a press conference. It's true that I worked with someone in our department when we handled press conferences, but I have also planned, organized and implemented at least fifteen press conferences that always exceeded the company's expectations. Would it help if I could give you an example or two?"

Most likely, he will say yes. Now you can give him a specific example of how your efforts exceeded expectations.

"Before teleconferencing was widely used, I suggested we hold a press conference for a statewide event via a teleconference so that more people could participate. It also made it easier for the press to cover it. This innovative way of holding a press conference became a news event in itself. All three TV stations were there, all the metropolitan papers and five radio stations reported on it, and we received a first place award from the National Association of Educational Public Relations."

BUT YOU DON'T EVEN KNOW ME

This is a good time to talk more about "preconceived notions." These are beliefs that an interviewer got in his head from some childhood experience at home or his fifth-grade teacher and probably wouldn't bring up in front of you. Depending on how the person views the world—in black and white or shades of gray—you may or may not be able to sway him to think differently.

A woman came up to me after a speech I had given and said, "I'm sixty-five years old and I know the reason I'm having trouble getting a new job is because of my age."

In this case, I asked her how she felt about bringing it up.

"Can I do that?" she asked.

"If you feel strongly it's an obstacle in the interviewer's mind but he's never going to bring it up, what do you have to lose?" I replied. Here's how I suggested she word it:

"I realize it may be a concern that I am more mature than most of the people you're talking to for this position. Let me assure you that, because of that, I bring a wealth of experience, a strong work ethic and loyalty to the firm I work for. I am committed to learning about your business and open to continuing education. In fact, I just completed my third computer class. I am also committed to being in this position for as long as we both feel it's a good match."

Another woman came up and asked me how to overcome her perceived liability—one that would definitely be a concern to an employer. She had left her career as a geologist ten years ago to raise her family. Now she wanted to reenter the job market and was concerned about this ten-year gap. Here's what she needed to do:

1. Figure out the prime concern on the employer's mind. The field of geology has changed dramatically in the last ten years, so her lack of updated knowledge is probably the biggest issue. Also, because she hasn't worked outside the home for awhile, there might be concern over her ability to be productive in this environment.

2. Take courses and read journals to update her skills and knowledge of the field and trends of the industry.

3. Be prepared to deal with this concern. Have an explanation ready that lists everything she's done to bring herself up-to-date and be a productive contributor. In fact, I wouldn't even wait until an employer brought it up. I'd include it as part of the information she shares early in the conversation or in correspondence.

What if it's a concern you weren't prepared for . . . something you never considered as a possible issue? For example, you're a female with loads of management experience and the interviewer says, "How do you feel about managing men?"

Ask yourself: What is he afraid of? Perhaps the last manager had difficulty with the men on the sales force. Perhaps the interviewer doesn't think women can manage men very well.

Reply with: "I feel fine about it. I've been a manager of both men and women for seventeen years and have always led them to be top achievers in every company I've worked for." You could end by asking, "Is there a reason you ask?"

Someone wrote to me once asking about this objection that had been raised by employers during his interviews:

"I have only worked for small companies. Interviewers have a perception that, because I have no experience in large corporations, I won't fit in."

If he looks at why employers feel this way, it will help him develop a case to quell these concerns. They might worry that:

1. He won't do well in a complex environment
2. He doesn't know how to deal with people at many different levels
3. He's not accustomed to dealing with many people

The solution is to tell how he:

- Has developed many responsibilities and dealt with many people outside the company—probably even more than someone in a large company

- Undoubtedly has broader experience, so he could be better qualified to work well in a complex environment and deal with all types of people
- Has an understanding of the big picture because he worked in and contributed to many areas of the small companies
- Has a keen understanding of the bottom line— he produces results

Again before any interview, think about:

- What characteristics and qualifications does the ideal candidate have?
- What is the interviewer afraid I *won't* have?
- How might the interviewer define my "type"? In other words, what preconceived notions will she have about me based on my background?

It only takes one experience of not being prepared. Once, I was interviewing for a staff position as a copywriter for an advertising agency after having been a freelance writer for six years. The creative director said, "Don't you think you'll have a difficult time working for somebody after you've been on your own for so long?"

Great question! I hadn't even thought about it. I was so busy thinking "I want this job" I never considered his concerns. This was one time spontaneity paid off. Without thinking, I said, "That's a good question." I was unknowingly doing step one: acknowledging his concern.

Then I said something like: "I think many people envision a freelance writer as working whenever he or she wants and being less committed than someone who works for a company. Even though I've been on my own, I'm very disciplined with my time, hold regular business hours, plus do whatever else it takes to get the job done. I'm very dedicated to doing the best job I can in any structure." With that, he offered me the position.

Part of your role in the interview is to clarify information that supports your qualifications or adds to the good impression you want to convey. When you hear an objection, don't hang your head in defeat. Objections aren't set in stone. They are issues of concern. Listen to the concern, acknowledge it, then show the interviewer why it's not an issue or how it can be resolved.

Then I Go and Spoil It All By Saying Something Stupid: Common Communication Blunders

Some things are sure to jinx the interview. The following are disastrous yet common communication blunders.

WOMEN AND MEN WHO LOVE TO TALK TOO MUCH

Minutia loses listeners and detracts from the importance of your message. Here's an example of how a public relations director responded to: "How did you handle the news about your company's recent layoff of 2,500 employees?"

DANGER ZONE

"That was just terrible. It was upsetting news for everyone. Well, the board had met in a private meeting the week before the news came out. The following Monday I was called into the president's office and given the news. He was upset too, but it was a decision that had to be made. I was surprised at the number, because we had been led to believe at a meeting two weeks earlier that the plant in Detroit wouldn't be affected. He wanted to keep it quiet; we talked for about a half an hour. He didn't want anything told to the press. After our meeting, I met with my staff. We met over lunch and throughout the entire afternoon. They were shocked. A few didn't want to work there anymore, they were so upset. I let them vent, because they really needed it. One man actually cried. We wrote down all the pros and cons of doing what management wanted. Then we came up with a plan that included sending news releases to the three TV stations, all eighteen radio stations and the two newspapers in town to announce a press conference. We felt it was important to have a press conference. I called back the president, who was at lunch; we met when he came back. In the meantime, I . . ."

Besides boring me with every iota of what she and her staff felt and did, this response tells me that she doesn't prioritize information in terms of relevance. I'm going to judge her communication skills by how she handles this question.

SAFE ZONE

"This was a very sensitive issue at our company because of the potential impact on the community in which our plant is located. I had two audiences to contend with: our senior management, who didn't want to make any announcement, and the press, of course. So I had to devise a strategy to deal with both. You see, I felt it was imperative to take a proactive approach. We had worked very hard to build an open and honest relationship with the media after that explosion took place six years ago. As soon as I was made aware of the company's position, I met with my staff to outline the potential hazards of that approach. I successfully persuaded senior management to follow our suggestions. As a result, all of the press we received was very fair and accurate, and to this day the company maintains a good relationship with the media."

This answer demonstrates her professionalism, sensitivity to her company and the public and willingness to take a stand, as well as her ability to be a team player and to persuade and lead with integrity and vision. Her ability to be precise and give relevant information affects my feelings about her capability to do the job.

SOUR GRAPES OF WRATH

Even subtle "sour grapes" attitudes come through loud and clear. This is not to be confused with what I touched on earlier when I talked about not discussing your anger about what the company "did" to you. I'm referring here to an *attitude* no matter what the subject is.

Here's an example that makes you wonder what the person was trying to hide.

This forty-nine-year-old man was in a workshop I was presenting. He was very concerned about how employers would view him. He kept telling the group that in his mind, his age was not a factor.

But when we reviewed what he'd say when asked why he left his last job, he replied, "The company had a downsizing and eliminated my job. I can't understand why they did it, but that's their decision and I just have to accept it. But I'm not ready for the rocking chair yet. Even at my age, I've still got a lot of kick in me and want a new challenge."

Listening to this man, do you hear resentment toward his company? What about the reference to his age? Even if it wasn't on your mind before, it would be now.

Another example of someone with an attitude problem was a woman who left her job for personal reasons. When we were practicing how she would handle the question she would surely hear, "Why did you leave your job?" she replied:

"In my opinion, the company was managed poorly and set as its priorities the expansion of its offices into the Latin countries instead of taking care of more urgent operations here. I often felt that the company insulted my intelligence by not listening to my suggestions."

Sometimes wrath is more overtly expressed. I know people who have used the interview to get back at their company or boss by bad-mouthing them or giving away company secrets.

SEX, LIES AND VIDEOTAPES

Monitoring what you share and don't share is especially crucial in a job interview.

In any conversation, you make decisions about what you say and don't say. You filter what is appropriate to share depending on who you're talking to, where you are and the topic at hand.

For example, common sense says that if you are attending a funeral, you're not going to sit there and talk about all the terrible things the deceased did in his lifetime or what a jerk you really thought he was.

If you give inappropriate information, an employer might think you are immature, lack social graces or can't be trusted in challenging or sensitive situations.

One of my clients was secretary to the company president. "Why do you want to leave your position?" I asked her. Here was her answer:

"My boss makes me stock his refrigerator every day with juices and all kinds of snacks. And when I'm not out shopping for him, I'm getting his car washed or on the phone to his wife making excuses about where he is. The guy is a nut."

I'm not the only one she told this to. This was her response to potential employers as well.

She probably has legitimate gripes. But is this appropriate information to share with her potential boss? How does it make her look? A secretarial position, in particular, calls for someone with good judgment, discretion and loyalty. Her answer does not sit well. Fair or not, the interviewer will make judgments about her ability to do the job based on what she conveys.

A manager told me about the time he was interviewing people to fill a sales position at his company. "I thought I had found just the right guy. Then he was telling me how he always tried to keep his expenses down when he was on the road by staying at inexpensive hotels. He said, 'I stay at the $29-a-night motels. That way I can go sit in the bar at the expensive hotels across the street and drink all night.' He laughed at the end of his story. I crossed him off my list."

The job candidate did himself in by sharing information that wasn't necessary and was definitely inappropriate in the eyes of this manager. And although the job hunter didn't know it, his last comment was particularly damaging because the manager was a recovering alcoholic.

Other people who had very brief interviews talked about their bad marriages, their sick mothers or children and other personal problems.

Not everyone shares your values and interests. Stay away from sensitive topics. It can damage your credibility in a split second.

ON TRIAL, YOU'RE NOT

Questions such as "Why is it taking you so long to find a new position?" or "What kind of trouble did you have with your last boss?" may ellicit a defensive reaction because they are negatively stated.

You might be tempted to answer this first question with: "The job market really stinks and no one seems to be interested in a fifty-two-year-old gray-haired engineer."

Don't buy into the negativity. Let them know you haven't been sitting around twiddling your thumbs.

A better way to handle this question: "I don't think it is taking me so long to find a new position. My company closed its doors four months ago. Since then, I have been assessing my strengths and researching the type of company where I could be most valuable. I have also been volunteering at our public TV station twice a week. I'm talking to many different people. I want my next position to be a good fit for both of us."

Phyllis, one of my clients, felt as if this interviewer was playing mind games with her when he asked questions from a negative angle.

"He said, 'I see here you had a 3.1 grade average at Notre Dame and a 3.7 at Boston University. Why didn't you excel at Notre Dame?' I was taken aback by his questions, but I answered him tactfully and didn't allow myself to be negative."

PASS THE BUCK

We've talked about salary as one of the elements that defines The Job You Want. But the potential problem with this whole money issue is that it can take on too much importance too early in the interview process.

I define too early as anytime before you're actually offered the position. If you discuss money before then, you are making money a criterion for the interviewer to use to decide if you get the job. You want to be offered the position because he thinks you're qualified for the position. Once you're offered the position, then you can discuss salary.

So don't bring it up. If he brings it up, do your best to postpone this discussion until it is appropriate. Say something like, "At this point I'd need to know more about the position. I'd feel more comfortable if we could hold off on any discussion of salary until I understand the needs of the position and we feel it's a good fit."

I'll get into more detail on this in chapter ten. For now, you need to know that talking about money can blow the interview and eliminate your chance to *ever* talk about it.

SUMMARY

Think of an interview as going out in public: Some things are OK to do and others aren't. Certain topics of discussion are acceptable and others are taboo. In an interview, you're holding a conversation to present yourself in the best possible light. Remember why you're there: to be considered for a position. What you say and how you say it will affect that.

CHECKLIST

✔ Avoid certain subjects such as bosses, people problems and personal issues.

✔ Don't sabotage the interview by believing

you're deficient or that the interviewer thinks you are.

✔ Be prepared for objections. Acknowledge and resolve them. They are an interviewer's fears that many times can be quelled—depending on what you say and how you say it.

✔ Don't talk too much.

✔ Don't go in with a hidden agenda to get back at the company you're with or worked for or make someone look bad.

✔ Turn around negatively stated questions.

CHAPTER 7

Elegant and Relevant

Strategy #7:

**Since you're the most qualified to
talk about you, make it good.**

So far I've talked a lot about what you *don't* want to say. Let's concentrate on what you *do* want to say.

In this chapter, I'll show you how to present yourself in a way that will knock an employer's socks off by sharing relevant, powerful information with brevity. Don't even think about skipping this part. I don't care if you have a Ph.D. in English or you're a nuclear physicist who gives presentations to other nuclear physicists, you—especially you—need help in this area.

Talking to someone who may be your next boss is a different ball game.

YOU'RE HALFWAY THERE

In chapter one, you figured out your *strengths* (unique talents and skills) by analyzing your accomplishments. You also identified your *expertise* and things you know about. That's all good stuff.

Here's the problem. You can have all the talent in the world, tell me about all the things you can do and know about, but I'm still taking a big risk by hiring you. I don't want to spend ten thousand to thirty thousand dollars to hire and train you only to find out six months later you were full of hot air. I want proof.

The proof is what I referred to in chapter two as your *potential*—one of the key elements employers scrutinize. They find it by looking at ways you have applied your strengths in past jobs and experiences. In other words, they want to know how you have made past employers productive and profitable, or made a difference in school or volunteer activities or as a homemaker.

This proof is what makes you valuable.

Now, I can't imagine most employers will sit there in an interview and say "Give me proof." Some may not even know that's what they want. What's more, most job hunters don't have the know-how or take the time to figure out this "proof." So when you do, believe me, you will be miles ahead of everyone else applying for the same job or exploring a way to create one.

Perhaps, without even knowing exactly how you did it, the employer will see you as a solution to his problems—just what the employer wants. Let's figure out your "proof" now. Grab some paper for the exercise that we'll be doing next.

THE PROOF IS IN YOUR PAST
Bring Back Old Memories

Think of specific, concrete examples from your past of how you used your strengths to solve problems to meet a company's needs or successfully complete a class or volunteer project.

You may be thinking that what you do isn't measurable. You wouldn't have your job, be able to manage a home or have graduated if you didn't create results. This list will help you.

HOW PEOPLE MAKE THINGS BETTER:

Organize something (new filing system, project, meetings, process)

Correct internal problems (payments, communication)

Handle double workload

Improve something (make it work or look better)

Create something

Increase or expand something

Increase new business

Reduce error rate

Obtain more information

Raise profile of company or event

Turn around a bad situation with a customer or client

Cut downtime

Get faster delivery time

Make the boss look good

Train staff on new procedure

Devise a new system and procedures

Avoid problems

Reduce inventory

Meet deadlines

Receive recognition

Cut operating costs

Track information

Increase customer satisfaction

Meet quality standards

Raise conformance ratings

Streamline a system

Eliminate sexual harassment claims

Are you thinking "Well, that's just part of the job" or "That's what I do"? That may be true, but these are also ways you made yourself valuable. Trust me. These are reasons that companies pay you to come to work every day. They show how you solve problems.

Put Pencil to Pad

Write each one down explaining:

- What the problem was
- What you did to try to solve it
- What the result was

Examples:

What the problem was: Our customer service department was not reacting quickly enough to customer complaints and problems. Most complaints took over fifteen days to get any response and we were losing business.

What I did to try to solve it: I reorganized our customer service department, created work teams and oversaw the cross-training of thirteen administrators.

What the result was: Customers were much happier and more satisfied, turnaround time for handling problems went from fifteen days to twenty-

four hours and employee morale increased dramatically.

Some of the strengths this person illustrated through this concrete example were her ability to:

1. Organize people, tasks and other facets of revamping an entire department
2. Oversee or take the lead in developing a training program
3. Present training of new policies, procedures and skills

What the problem was: I was an active volunteer in Amnesty International at a time when dozens of people were being held as political prisoners in a particular country.

What I did to try to solve it: I coordinated and implemented a letter-writing campaign and fundraiser.

What the result was: Our efforts led to the eventual release of these political prisoners.

I realize there is a lot more to your accomplishments than this simplified explanation. You can go into greater detail if the interviewer wants to know more. But for now, you need to be able to cite specific, concise examples of how you used your strengths in the past. It is hard to be concise; that's why you need to practice before you go into the interview. What you're showing your potential employer is your potential—which can be "proved" by your past. You need to do this effectively.

Write down as many examples as you can think of.

Which sounds more interesting to you?

1. I have a lot of experience in training people and am very effective.

2. When our company product line went from typewriters to computers, we had a very seasoned sales force but they didn't know the first thing about computers. I was in charge of training our U.S. sales representatives, plus our people in Canada and Mexico, and within three months had converted the entire sales force into experts on this newer technology. This was the beginning of establishing ourselves as leaders in this industry.

Obviously, the answer is 2. What makes it interesting? It's a specific example and it's a story. People remember stories. It helps them apply what you're saying. When this job hunter leaves the interview, the employer will remember her as "the trainer who converted an entire sales force into experts on new technology."

Present Your "Proof" When the Interviewer Asks:

- "Can you give me an example?"
- "What are your strengths?" Give a strength and support it with an example.
- "What's a difficult situation that you turned around?"
- "Tell me about a time you . . ."

In general, anytime you're explaining something, if you have an example, use it. Follow the format of describing the problem, what you did and what the result was.

Don't Forget the Result!

When I role-play interviews with my clients, they tend to leave out this third and important part of the story. Here's a way to help you remember.

Practice your interview skills with someone and ask them to apply the *"So What? Rule."* When you make a statement about something you did, do you explain why it was significant? Do you tell how it made a difference? Tell your coach to listen for that. If you didn't give it, have her say "So what?"

Like my clients who I make practice this rule, you'll probably feel annoyed at first as someone sits there and demands "So what?" every time you say something.

It's a bit like Pavlov's theory on conditioned reflex. You make a statement and your coach says "So what?" After a few irritating times, you'll associate anything you say with "So what?" and you'll start supporting your statements without being prodded. This will make you very effective in interviews.

Some people insist their work is not measurable or quantifiable. James is a diversity expert who had an interview with a company on the East Coast. The interviewer asked him to translate his work into meaningful information. James told her how it was important for everyone to be able to get along in an organization and to accept and value peoples'

differences. "But how does this impact the bottom line?" she insisted.

For James, that wasn't the important issue. He hadn't thought it out. In fact, he felt the interviewer's mind-set demonstrated a clash with his values. It's possible the interviewer thought so as well, since James was not offered the position.

If James did want to be on the same wavelength with the interviewer, he needed to talk about how his diversity-training classes had contributed to the decrease in sexual harassment claims, increased productivity and encouraged teamwork.

See how much better you sound?

Coming up with your proof and putting it in this format is a tough assignment. Just think of what you would have sounded like before you did that difficult but enlightening exercise (see page 63).

WHAT DO YOU KNOW—LET'S REVIEW

If you completed all nine exercises in chapter one and this last one, you now know:

1. Your strengths
2. Your personal characteristics
3. What challenges you
4. Your worth
5. Environments that suit your personality, style, interest and values
6. Your values
7. Businesses you believe in and support
8. How you like to be recognized by management
9. Your knowledge
10. How you have benefited past employers and how you can be of value to another company

Now you're ready to take the relevant facts from this and put them into a concise, powerful presentation.

Why is this important? In the interview, you'll be evaluated according to your ability to communicate. Interviewers are listening to see if you share information in a positive, well-organized and clear fashion.

Start listening to other people in casual conversations and business settings with a more critical ear. You'll notice that the more articulate the person, the more credible he is. But if he rambles, is negative or confusing, the faster you want to get away from him.

QUESTION	B.E. (BEFORE ENLIGHTENMENT)	A.E. (AFTER ENLIGHTENMENT)
What is your greatest achievement?	Um, let's see, I guess it's graduating from college . . . raising our two children . . . the last two promotions I received . . . I guess I'd have to think about it.	My greatest achievement in my career has been the project I just completed, in which I developed and implemented the re-engineering program of our 125–staff division. We had to make drastic cuts in our operations due to a new directive from top management. The program I designed cut costs by $2.5 million annually without laying off a single employee.
How will you keep two hundred sales reps updated on new products?	Well, I'd probably develop some type of program where I had regular contact with them . . . something like a weekly newsletter or bulletin. I'd hold a sales meeting twice a year at the home office . . .	I can give you an example of how I did that in my last position, in which I oversaw a national sales force of three hundred reps. I developed a monthly video program which was sent to each office in the country, where the reps would watch it at their monthly meetings. I also developed a weekly bulletin that covered the most frequently asked customer questions, complaints and service issues and how to handle them. Because of this frequent, consistent and thorough communication program, we cut the number of our national meetings in half, saving the company $800,000 the first year. Plus, our national sales increased 30 percent.
How have you been successful?	Well, I've handled some of the biggest projects in this field with great success, overseeing divisional and regional affairs and tracking two capital projects and receiving national recognition for my work.	I oversaw the first international computer operations program that established a strategic direction for our company's mainframe computers. I worked with our staff in every country, and within six months we had global contracts and had standardized our hardware and software processes.

It takes practice and a certain mind-set to quickly synthesize relevant information and present it in a logical and brief format. During my radio program, listeners call up and ask questions. Before they get on the air, my phone screener asks them their question and tells them to be prepared to state it. Even then, most of them get on the air, I listen patiently as they talk for awhile and a little while longer, and eventually I need to say "What's the question?" "Oh yeah," they say, and then come back with more details. Again, I say "So what's the question?"

In the case of your job search, though, you do have time to think through what you want to say and how you're going to say it. In fact, you must think it through if you want to sound credible and professional.

You started putting this information into a logical format in chapter four when you wrote your:

- *Personal Overview* (your strengths and overview of expertise and experience)
- *Reason for job hunting* (positive explanation of what has happened in your career to put you in the job market)
- *Career objective* (explanation of what you want to move toward and how you can contribute)

Now you're ready to take this information and put it into the form of a three-minute commercial. People have short attention spans, and they shouldn't have to work to figure out what you mean. Your commercial will aid listeners. They will like you and admire you for it.

YOUR THREE-MINUTE COMMERCIAL

This is a well-thought-out, brief, rehearsed presentation of who you are, what you're looking for, why you're in the situation you're in, and why someone would want to hire you—not necessarily in that order. You can use this presentation in its entirety, but most of the time you'll use the parts that are relevant in these kinds of situations:

- In response to the interviewer when she says "Tell me about yourself"
- When you meet someone in a professional setting
- When someone asks you about yourself in a social setting

The best way to create your three-minute commercial is to follow an outline such as this:

1. **Brief overview of where you've been**
   A. Your area of expertise, background and knowledge
   B. Why you're looking for a job

2. **Your objective**
   A. Industries or areas you're exploring
   B. What kind of position you're looking for
   C. If this is a career change, brief explanation of how your skills transfer and why you're interested in this field

3. **More details on you**
   A. Your strengths
   B. Your experience (positions and overview of responsibilities)
   C. Specific accomplishments (ways you've been valuable) that illustrate how you've applied your strengths

4. **Education if relevant and/or recent**

5. **Recap of your objective**

Yes, you can get all that into about three minutes. It can even be shorter. Use three minutes as a guide.

I highly recommend this outline approach and caution against writing your three-minute commercial out word-for-word. The outline will keep it from becoming:

1. A crutch (You'll become dependent on it and this is not something you're going to be sitting there reading.)
2. Something you'll end up memorizing (It will sound rehearsed and insincere.)
3. A source of frustration (If memorized, you'll expect yourself to always say it exactly as you wrote it. If you lose your place or forget something, you'll feel you did poorly.)

Write down the key points to support your outline. Then say it out loud. Practice. Record yourself on tape. Time yourself. Ask someone to listen. Ask for feedback. This forces you to give only relevant information, to be specific and brief.

You may think a three-minute commercial wouldn't have much application in a social setting.

But what do people talk about in social situations? One of the first questions is usually "What do you do?" This will help you discuss your present job, if you're employed, and your other job—looking for one. You never know who is hiring or knows someone who is. This exercise will help you be as articulate as possible at all times.

I can just see it now. I'll get bushels of mail from people saying "I tried out my three-minute commercial at a cocktail party and people were literally running away from me. You've ruined my social life."

No wonder. People go to cocktail parties for six reasons:

1. To be seen
2. To see who's who, who's worth knowing and if they can meet them
3. To eat free food
4. To drink free drinks
5. To meet people who may be able to help them in their career, increase their business, give them information, help them make more money or give them advice
6. Simply to socialize

With that in mind, would you stick around to listen to someone's three-minute commercial? Neither will they.

So when you are introduced to John Hancock, president of Hancock Insurance, at an art opening, and he says, "So what do you do, Beverly?", don't launch into:

"I work for the Goodman Printing Company as a sales representative. I have ten years experience in sales and marketing with a successful track record. I particularly enjoy client contact where I get the opportunity to apply my strengths, which are my ability to build trusting relationships, communicate clearly, apply my in-depth knowledge of the printing industry, create strategic marketing programs and give persuasive sales presentations."

Simply answer the man's question. "I'm a sales representative for the largest and most successful printing firm in Los Angeles."

"Oh," Mr. Hancock will politely reply—and will either know who that is or ask "Who is that?"

Now you're having a conversation, not a one-sided sales pitch.

The key is knowing your material and being able to use it when and where it's appropriate.

When I give a speech, I do not stand up there and rattle off every single thing I know. I know my subject inside out, backward, forward and sideways. So when I'm up there, depending on my audience, I present what's pertinent, concentrating on *how* I'm saying it and if the audience is getting it.

It's the same thing with your material. If you know the content, it becomes second nature. You won't have to tell every point. You bring up what's relevant at the time. That's having a conversation.

So, social setting or not, you don't necessarily want to use your commercial in its entirety. Go with the flow. Use the elements to hold a conversation.

In an actual interview, though, the components of a three-minute commercial will be points an interviewer will undoubtedly ask. You may end up revealing only parts of it at the appropriate times rather than all at once. Either way, you will be well prepared.

SAMPLE THREE-MINUTE COMMERCIALS:
Operations/Management:

I have seventeen years in operations and management, mostly in the pharmaceutical industry. My company just went through a restructuring. My position, along with forty others, was eliminated. I'm disappointed about this and enjoyed my time at the Biaxial Company. However, I'm looking at this as an opportunity to take my years of experience and knowledge in operations and management to another firm, either in the same industry or another manufacturing environment.

My objective is to find a position where I can contribute my skills as a problem solver, planner and an effective communicator, and my ability to motivate others to meet their goals and objectives. I have a proven track record with Biaxial as vice president of operations; before that I was with the Bill & Jean Company as operations manager. My responsibilities at Biaxial included overseeing the daily operations of a multimillion dollar plant, developing new policies and procedures for our production facilities and working closely with all departments, including marketing, quality control and information systems.

An example of how I've used my skills success-

3-MINUTE COMMERCIAL EXAMPLE

Why she's looking for a new position:	"My company just went through a restructuring. My position, along with forty others, was eliminated. I'm disappointed about this loss, and enjoyed my fifteen years at the Rose Company. However, I'm looking at this as an opportunity to offer my years of experience and knowledge in operations and management to another company.
Her ojective, strengths and overview of her career and expertise:	"Now my objective is to find a position where I can contribute my skills as a problem solver, planner, trainer and an effective communicator and my ability to motivate others. I have a total of eighteen years experience. Specifically, I worked for the Rose Company as vice president of operations; before that I was with the Arthur Company as operations manager.
What she has to offer an employer in terms of strengths and accomplishments:	"An example of how I've used my skills successfully is when I planned and organized an innovative purchasing system for five of our stores, saving $70,000 in one year. I feel that my strengths will allow me to successfully manage the daily operations of a business and I have a proven track record of doing that by keeping an eye on the bottom line and building on people's strengths.
Recap or rephrasing of her objective:	"I've analyzed what I want to do next and it's important for me to be very involved in the hands-on operations of a company and to see firsthand how I help a company grow. As a matter of fact, one thing I'd like to do is be involved with a start-up company."

fully is when I planned and organized a new distribution system for five of our plants, saving $1.5 million in one year.

I feel confident that my strengths will allow me to successfully manage the daily operations of another manufacturing business. I want to be involved in the daily operations of a company and to be able to see firsthand how I make a difference.

Recent Graduate:

I just completed my Masters degree in health services administration, with a concentration in long-term care, from Xavier University. Prior to that I received my B.A. degree in psychology from the University of Notre Dame.

Besides my education, I have hands-on experience in the United States and abroad. Last fall I completed an internship with Berwick Retirement Community as an administrative resident. I assisted the administrator in daily operations of this fifty-five-bed skilled nursing unit and one hundred-apartment assisted living wing. This experience confirmed my passion for working with the elderly and gave me firsthand knowledge of how operations, finances and quality care work together. The previous year, through the International Youth Exchange, I was a nurse assistant at a nursing home in Holland. I assisted with the daily care and transportation of residents.

I have always had great empathy and appreciation for mature adults, having been a volunteer for Meals on Wheels and a nursing home aid since I was a teenager. These experiences have enhanced my strengths, which are: planning, organizing and coordinating procedures and systems, initiating and following through on complex projects, training and working well with management and staff.

For example, when I was at the retirement home here, I trained administrative and nursing staff on the value of generating and tracking statistical data in a spreadsheet format. Until then, they were getting information from various sources and it was not accurate. As a result, the home now has accurate quality assurance tools to determine residents' health.

I feel my interest in this area, my strong education and strengths can contribute greatly to the overall efficiency and smooth operations of a health care organization.

Technical Sales and Product Management:

I have a total of fourteen years experience, nine years in technical sales and five years in product management. Most of that was spent in the chemical and cosmetic industries.

I'm in the process of looking for a new position since my firm will be moving its operations to Dallas and I am not in a position to transfer. I would like to contribute my strengths in developing customer relationships, negotiating, solving distribution, marketing and pricing problems, analyzing new business opportunities and organizing the introduction of new products into the marketplace.

I am results-oriented and my past performance demonstrates my ability to meet or exceed sales goals. For example, in less than one year, I increased sales in a stagnant territory by 25 percent. I developed new business worth fifteen million dollars when the company expanded to the West Coast.

I am also very knowledgeable about sales forecasting, specification sales, national account contact, territory layout and management.

Communications and Nonprofit:

I recently moved to this area when my wife took a position at University Hospital. Now that we're settled, I am exploring this market for a position that will build upon my expertise and knowledge in marketing communications and nonprofit organizations.

Before we came to the Midwest, I was product marketing manager for Dora Industries in Atlanta. I developed and implemented marketing programs for its financial services products. I also supported a field sales organization of fifteen hundred with product information and managed and coordinated internal marketing communications.

I have developed expertise in fund-raising and grant writing, having been very active in community service. Through my work as a volunteer and outreach consultant to Big Brothers, Jaycees and working with inner-city youth, I planned and directed several pilot programs that are now used by the national organizations.

My strengths include planning and overseeing complex projects, working with teams to accomplish goals, and my ability to resolve problems related to human resources and communication issues.

I recently finished my Masters degree in community social psychology, and now would like to find a nonprofit organization that can benefit from my strong communications and marketing background.

Senior Executive:

I have nineteen years in this industry with a successful profit-making track record. I've managed the nuts and bolts of every operation in this business. My expertise has been honed at my job at Joye Industries in operations, accounting, planning and new product development. I'm proud to have been a part of an organization that has gone from seventh place to being the leader in this industry in just four years.

As a member of senior management, I've been instrumental in the strategic planning and restructuring of our company. I attribute my success to my focus on the bottom line, commitment to meeting goals, my blend of analytical and intuitive thinking and my ability to garner support from staff.

For example, I planned and implemented our restructuring program, which will save the company twenty-two million dollars over the next year. We've already seen the results through a significant improvement in our customer service.

I have been instrumental in making us the leader in our industry, and am ready to face a similar challenge in another company in this part of the country. My objective is to oversee the day-to-day operations and strategic planning of a firm to improve profit and growth. I will do that by contributing my extensive knowledge of the industry and proven record in finances, planning and new product development.

Homemaker Re-entering the Workforce:

For the past eight years I've managed our home and the daily activities of our two children and planned and prepared meals to meet our family's nutritional requirements. I have had the opportunity to implement many of my strengths in this environment and am proud of the many contributions I've made to our community.

For example, I've been very active in our school system as Board president. I organized the first city-wide multicultural program for our district. The program was so successful, it's now the pilot program for school districts across the state. I also organized the school's Parent Teacher Organization, which led to the purchase of needed computers and updated gym facilities.

I initiated a neighborhood block watch, in which I write a monthly newsletter, as well as plan, coordinate and run our meetings. I've been instrumental in cutting the crime rate on our street because of the programs the block watch has implemented.

All of these illustrate my strengths as an effective planner, promoter, writer, organizer and leader. Prior to this role, I was a teacher in the Southwestern County Schools and New London Local Schools and communications director for the St. Paul Orphanage. My objective now is to get back into the workforce in a position where I can coordinate special events and promote the benefits of a valuable service.

Natural, Not Rehearsed

Now you may not identify with any of the positions I've used as examples. But what was your im-

pression of what each person had to say? Each one sounded confident, credible, focused and like somebody you'd want on your team, right?

Each one of these people was just like you before they developed their three-minute commercial. But they spent time—many hours—organizing this information.

FIVE RULES OF ELEGANCE
Listen to the Question

The worst thing you can do is answer a question you didn't hear or understand. I had a client who got so nervous during interviews, he didn't listen to the question, tried to answer it, and as a result left interviewers totally perplexed. They thought he was either stupid or had a hearing problem.

If you didn't hear or understand something, ask for clarification.

Also, make sure the interviewer even *asks* a question.

One of my clients told me, "This man who got my resumé called me up to talk and I think I blew it. I revealed way too much information."

When I asked her what she had told him, she said, "I told him about my last two jobs and why I was looking and what I wanted to do next."

"What was the question that he asked you?" I asked her.

She looked at me and said, "He didn't ask me anything. All he did was tell me about the opening and I just went on and on."

Only Offer Information That Answers the Question

If the question is "Why did you leave your last job?" don't say:

"I've never really felt comfortable there, because they had me doing bookkeeping work when I wasn't hired to do that. But I hadn't planned to leave. I would have stayed. My husband just got transferred here, and I need a new job."

The only information she needs to give to answer the question is:

"I recently moved here to join my family. My husband's company opened a new office here and he was transferred to manage it."

Think Through and Share Relevant Facts

If you're asked how you handled that problem customer, don't say:

"What a jerk! I couldn't believe he refused to leave and then called security. I was a little shook up at first. I've never dealt with anyone like that. But then I remembered the training we had on dealing with an abusive customer and I asked him what he would like me to do at this point."

The relevant facts are:

"When the man refused to leave, I recalled the training I had just undergone and stated in a low voice, 'Sir, what would you like me to do at this point?' He calmed down and I was able to handle the transaction to his satisfaction. He was no longer threatening and a potentially negative situation was totally turned around."

Take Time to Pause or Reflect Before You Answer a Question

A little silence is OK. You want to sound sincere, not rehearsed. So stop and think before you give an answer. If you need time to gather your thoughts, you can say "Let me think about that a second" or "That's a good question"—while your mind is quickly assessing the appropriate response.

Only Share Positive Information

I think I've said enough on that. But in addition, here are the kinds of topics and information that you may not think to share, but that can be very positive.

• The career consultant who told about his involvement in a minor league baseball league. This showed balance and his ability to get along with others.
• The man who had been out of work for four months who volunteered at the public TV station. This showed that he was using his time off productively and was a giving person.
• My clients who have just graduated from college and don't have work experience have told about times they volunteered for committees and community groups, were officers in their fraternity or sorority, led class projects, acted in plays and sang in choruses. These illustrate balance, leadership, ability to get along with others and experience with teams.
• To demonstrate a lifetime of success and leadership roles, my forty-five-year-old client shared how he had been active in sports, was captain of his basketball team, an officer on the school council and president of his fraternity throughout high school and college.

Tips:
Steer Clear of "Always" and "Never"

Sentences that use absolutes are hard to prove.

Use Non-sexist Language

Examples:

Sexist word	*Replacement*
Businessman	Business executive
Man-hours	Worker hours
Workmen	Workers
Salesmen	Salespeople
Chairman	Chairperson

Get With It

Update your language so you don't sound ill-informed, old-fashioned, bigoted or sexist. I'm not suggesting you only use the politically correct phrase. Just don't use terminology that is condescending and judgmental. Examples:

Inappropriate	*Appropriate*
Superior	Boss, manager
Girls	Women
The wife	Spouse or my wife
Handicapped	Disabled
Women's libber	Feminist
Housewife	Works out of the home

No Four-letter or Crude Words

You know what profanity is. But I've noticed how phrases such as "pissed off" and "it sucks" have made their way into acceptable everyday speech. They are crude.

Ain't Gonna Have No Bad Grammar

Sometimes I wonder if everybody was sick the day their grammar teacher taught the proper usage of the English language. (I know I was sick the day they taught fractions.) All right, maybe I'm exaggerating. But the language used in conversations and letters by some people should be banished from this Earth. Common mistakes I hear:

No such word or phrase	What you mean
Orientated	Oriented
Simular	Similar
Yous	You
I had went	I had gone
Irregardless	Regardless
I seen	I have seen or I saw
Pacific	Specific

He Who Hesitates Is Lost

Don't use phrases that make you sound unsure, indecisive or noncommittal. Examples:

Tentative	Just say what you mean
I guess I learned that when . . .	I learned that when . . .
I think my strengths are . . .	My strengths are . . .
I'll try. . .	I will . . .
I probably . . . maybe . . . could . . .	I will . . .
Basically, I think . . .	I think . . .

What a Snob

These phrases sound snooty:
It appears that . . .
It should be noted that . . .
It can be stated that . . .
It goes without saying that . . .
General rule: Just say whatever "it" is.

Be Active, Not Passive

The active voice is not only easier to understand than the passive voice, it puts emphasis on what you did.

Passive	Active
The first teleconference in the state was organized by me.	I organized the first teleconference in the state.

No Valley Girls

They complete their sentences with "I'm like" and say "he goes." When you do that you sound ineffective and immature.

Valspeak	Professionalspeak
There was this customer who's screaming at me, and I'm like, what now? Do I, like, hang up? So then, I remember, oh yeah, you're supposed to, like, take a deep breath and say . . .	A customer on the phone became very irate and began screaming at me. At first I was shocked because this had never happened. Then I recalled what we learned in our training session . . .
When I asked what the problem was, he goes . . .	When I asked what the problem was, he said . . .

The "I" Word Is Not Naughty

It may feel unnatural to say "I did this or that" when talking about your work—as if you are bragging. So be aware of the tendency to say "we" as opposed to "I." You're not in an interview to promote your department or company.

Tendency	Replace with
We developed a new process.	I was instrumental in developing a new process.
We came up with a new design.	I was part of the team that came up with the new design.

Turnoffs

Pay attention to your speech pattern, pitch and tone. It's very annoying when people talk too loudly, too softly, too fast, mumble or have heavy accents. If you do have an accent and people have difficulty understanding you, think about investing in a speech therapist to soften—not necessarily delete—your accent.

Buzz Words That Lack Substance

"Win-win" and "empowerment" are examples of tired phrases that people use to describe complex business issues. Use your own words to describe what you mean.

Jargon Is Jive

You lose your listener when you use language that only a colleague in your industry or your company understands. It ostracizes people. He may even feel embarrassed that he should know what you're talking about. Jargon includes:

Technobabble

auto-immune diagnostics	high-level language interface
isolation and purification procedures	multi-user systems development
conversion migration	electrogalvanizing line
	ANSI/ASQC
	visual Basic

Companyspeak (language specific to that particular company)

interface	employee deployment
computing category	people systems
reformatting module	drove the transition
new hire on-boarding	competitor product
provide productivity tools	cross-reference
	specialized stats
promotion analysis methodology	deliverables
	consensus proposal
service level objectives	emergency extraction

Industry jargon

mold and part design	intervener discovery
large instrument systems	masthead
	scraping down
holdout	Greek fold
pull-through marketing programs	intermediary access sale
	pinx
	second levels
bulk gas-distribution piping systems	standards and measurement criteria
rate rebalancing	

Acronyms: Insider Information
Walk into a meeting sometime of a company that uses acronyms to describe internal departments, methodology and programs and you'll feel like you're visiting a foreign land. For example:

"My POV on this is that it's the wrong thing for the MSD. And when it comes to LA, using the trainers is our CBA."

See what I mean? In case you're wondering, POV means "point of view"; MSD stands for Management Systems Development department; LA is Latin American market; CBA is "current best approach." This language might be fine to use at your company, but not on job interviews.

General rule: Since you will probably talk with many different types of people in a job search— some who may know exactly what you do and others who don't—when you talk, pretend you're talking to your mother.

Words and Phrases to Know and Use:

team	dialogue
leadership	human relations
quality	vision
multicultural	values

SUMMARY
Actress Ruth Gordon said: "The best impromptu speeches are those written well in advance." "Write" your presentation well in advance and you'll sound impromptu and more credible.

CHECKLIST
✔ Organize your thoughts.
✔ Know what you want to communicate, create an outline and practice.
✔ Pick relevant information that creates a picture in the listener's mind.
✔ Arm yourself with specific examples of why you're valuable.
✔ Create a credible and professional summary of the facts in three minutes or less.
✔ Brush up on your grammar and current language usage.
✔ Always be prepared to talk about yourself, your contributions and goals.
✔ Understand that you are not bragging, but are the one best qualified to talk about yourself.
✔ Be a good listener.
✔ Speak in terms that are important to the company and responsive to the questions asked.
✔ Translate jargon into people-oriented terminology.
✔ Be a storyteller.

CHAPTER 8

It's A Phase You're Going Through

Strategy #8

Interpret and identify each phase of the interview so you know when to do what.

Now we get down to the nitty-gritty. Let's discuss the stages and phases of an actual interview, how to follow up and what you can do to move the process along or end it. Yes, *end* it—if you decide at some point the job's not for you.

Here you'll learn the specifics. You're going to see how everything you've learned so far fits into the interview: When do you listen? When do you ask questions? When do you give your three-minute commercial? How do you follow up without being a pest? This is the When You Do What chapter.

First I'll talk about the sequence of events—from a screening interview to a third interview—and the goal of each phase.

Then I'll get specific and talk about the actual parts of an interview.

I picture the interview in seven parts. The parts may not always happen exactly in this order. They will vary depending on the stage—whether it's a first, second or third interview and who you're talking to.

In general, the following information and the seven steps are the natural chain of events. Some parts may be repeated in second and third interviews. This will become clear as you go along.

FIRST, SECOND AND THIRD INTERVIEWS
In the Beginning: The First Interview

Companies hold the initial interview (also called screening interview) to find out if you would be successful in this job.

Someone in the personnel department screens you if it's a large corporation and you got in the door through an ad in the paper, a recruiter or an opening you heard about from someone.

In a smaller company, you could meet with the hiring manager or an assistant in the department where you'd work. The larger the company, the more structured the process. If a company is flying you into town for an interview, you will most likely meet with more than one person.

Their goal is to decide whether you get a second interview, either with the manager or supervisor you'd work for, with some of the same people or with new ones.

If you're talking to someone from personnel, don't bore him with a lot of technical details unless he asks. His job is to decide if there is a fit with the job and the organization: Do you have the necessary skills, education and attitude? Talk in more general terms.

Your goal is to get invited to the second interview (if you've decided the position is a good fit based on what you know so far). Later in this chapter I will talk about how to gracefully drop out of the process at any point you decide you don't want to pursue the job.

HOW TO ACHIEVE YOUR GOAL
• Make a great first impression.

I bet my bottom dollar that Emily Post would tell

you a good conversationalist is someone who shows sincere interest in people. And that's exactly what you want to do when talking to interviewers. Here's how.

If you're exploring whether this is a good match rather than trying to sell yourself, this naturally takes place. You simply cannot accomplish this exploration if you're not sincere in wanting to know more about the person, his needs and what he wants to know. Listen to what he says, his tone of voice and watch his eyes and facial expressions.

Respond to clues you pick up from words and nonverbal communication. If you are attuned to this, you will be involved in the conversation.

• Find out what he's looking for by listening carefully to the job description.

Take mental notes and then share the kind of information that demonstrates your ability to do the job.

• When you talk, use language from the core competencies I discussed in chapter two.

Use key words from the job description if you saw it in advance.

• Don't just rehash what's on your resumé.

And in response to a question, definitely don't say "That's on my resumé." The same client I told you about in chapter two, who attached his resumé instead of completing my forms, did that during interviews. He felt it was the interviewer's responsibility to have thoroughly read his resumé beforehand. He came across as controlling and impatient. I've had other clients who just assumed the interviewer knew their resumé inside out. They were naive.

It is not the interviewer's responsibility to go through your resumé with a fine-toothed comb. Some might. Some don't even get a chance to read it before the interview. But it is *your* responsibility to show the interviewer the person behind that piece of paper.

• Know where you stand when you leave.

At the end, say: "I've enjoyed learning more about your company and this position. What is the next step?"

She could say:

1. "We'll be in touch," to which you reply: "If I haven't heard back from you by March 15, may I call you?"

2. "You'll be getting a call from Ms. Gutierrez' department to set up a meeting with her," to which you reply: "Terrific. When do you think I can expect to hear from her?"

3. (Highly unlikely, but possible) "I don't think this is a good match, but thanks for your interest," to which you reply: "Could you tell me what makes you feel that way?" She may not be willing to say much. But it's an opportunity to get valuable feedback.

All of these responses help you know where you stand and what to expect next. That helps you direct your energy, structure your follow-up and make efficient use of your time. You're also not left wondering what they thought and why you haven't heard back, which is *not* efficient use of your time.

You could be asked to take the kinds of tests covered in chapter two.

If you do poorly on tests, they could decide that's a reason not to hire you. You can ask companies for the results of your tests, but for legal reasons they will probably shy away from giving you actual scores. If you do ask, wait until the process is complete and you know whether or not you got the position.

Round Two: The Second Interview

If you get a second interview, you're being considered for the position. You'll most likely meet with someone or several people you'd work with in the department or the person you'd report to. It's hard to predict exactly what will happen. But they will definitely examine you more closely.

One employer told me that at this stage he looks for reasons to eliminate people. Depending on the position and who you met with in the first interview, you could get an offer.

Their goals are to decide if you have the technical skills and knowledge to do the job; look for evidence of your attitudes about people and things and how well you'd get along in the department or organization; learn about your potential to make the company better or more profitable.

Your goal is to decide if you want to continue

the process. Do you have the necessary skills for the position? How well do you think you'd get along there? What are the problems you'd deal with and how would you contribute? Are your values in alignment with the company's? If you like what you've heard so far, your goal is to get invited to a third interview.

HOW TO ACHIEVE YOUR GOAL:

• Find out in greater detail what they're looking for and tell them about your education, experience, strengths and specific examples that demonstrate your ability to do the job.

• Be pleasant, enthusiastic, diplomatic, cooperative and confident.

• Share concrete examples of problems you've faced in past jobs, what you did to solve them and the results of your efforts. (How much money did you save? How much waste did you cut? How much was efficiency or effectiveness improved?)

• Know where you stand before you leave. Watch for the interviewer's reaction. If you can't read her, or nothing is said about the next step, say: "I feel very good about what I learned and that my background and qualifications are closely matched to this position. Would you agree?"

She could say:

1. "Yes, I do. I'd like you to come back and meet with our Vice President of Sales, Sam Kaufman. What's your schedule like Tuesday?" to which you reply: "Terrific. I could meet anytime in the morning."

2. "I think you have a lot of the skills we're looking for, but I'm concerned about your lack of business-to-business sales experience," to which you reply: "What specifically concerns you about that?" This is your chance to deal with her concern and demonstrate it's not a problem.

3. "Yes, I think you're qualified," to which you reply: "Then does it make sense to set up another interview?" If she says yes, great. If she says, "We're talking to several other candidates, so I'll be back in touch," respond with: "If I haven't heard from you by March 15, may I call you to see where you are in the process?"

Getting Serious: The Third Interview

If you get a third interview, you're being *seriously* considered for the position. You could be talking to the same people you met in the second round, a new crew comprised of peers or other managers, or the decision-maker these people report to.

Their goals are to weigh all the information they have or verify what they've heard about you and delve deeper into how you think, feel and react to situations; to sell you on the job.

They may talk about benefits, the city—if you're relocating—and give you more insight into the company. You'll sense they may even let their guard down to lure you in by sharing information about a project you'd work on. They could introduce you to other people.

Your goal is to weigh all the information you have to determine if the position is still a good match. Do you know for sure who you would be working for? If there's any question about this, make sure you meet this person. If everything still seems on target, reaffirm the good impression you've obviously made so far and get the offer (if it's the last interview), or go to the next step.

HOW YOU ACHIEVE YOUR GOAL:

• Summarize your feelings about the position, your interest in working on the projects they've described and your ability to do a successful job.

• Depending on where you are in the process, this might be a good time to write and present an outline of what you can do for the company (examples come later in this chapter).

• If timing is right and you feel comfortable doing it, ask for the job.

• At least ask about the next step.

• Depending on what she says, ask if it's OK to check back.

Some of my clients have had between two and eight interviews before they were offered the position or were eliminated from the running. Stages will vary according to the company and how it operates, and the position under consideration.

THE SEVEN PHASES OF A JOB INTERVIEW

PHASE 1:

YOU'RE BOTH GETTING COMFY
- Establish rapport
- Cover the agenda

PHASE 2:

YOU GET TO KNOW THEM;
THEY GET TO KNOW YOU
- Listen
- Discover their needs
- Let them know what you've got
- Ask questions
- Clarify

PHASE 3:

THEY'RE GETTING TO KNOW ALL ABOUT YOU
- Illustrate how you can help solve their problems

PHASE 4:

YOU DEAL WITH THE "BUTS"
- Overcome objections

PHASE 5:

COME TO SMOOTH CONCLUSIONS
- Tie up loose ends
- Confirm their interest
- End on a good note

PHASE 6:

WHERE DO WE GO FROM HERE?
- Set up the next step

PHASE 7:

GIVE THANKS
- Write thank-you note(s)
- Send proposal

PHASE 1: GETTING COMFY
I'm OK, Are You OK?

When you meet someone—whether it's for the first time or you've been pals since sixth grade—there's an initial "meet and greet" ceremonial dance that takes place. It sets the tone and helps everyone get comfortable.

"David, how are you? I haven't seen you in ages! What have you been up to?"

or

"Hello, Daniel, it's nice to meet you. Would you like an iced tea? Some spring water?"

In an interview, it can include the exchange of similar pleasantries, such as, "How are you?" "How was your flight?" "Did you find us OK?" "May I take your coat?" "Were the directions OK?" or "Would you like some coffee?" This is the first part of *establishing rapport.*

First Impressions

Interviewers want to put you at ease and also see the real you. So they may start off by asking these kinds of questions, which are easy to answer and help you relax.

But don't let it all hang out. Stay on guard, because the interview has already begun. It started the second she set eyes on you. Smile, give a firm handshake, look the interviewer in the eye and let her take control. In the first seven to ten seconds of this initial meeting, people can pick up a lot of information. Fair or not, the impression you make in those first seconds can be a lasting one.

I once read that one in five interviewers decides on a job candidate in the first five minutes, and two-thirds need only fifteen minutes.

In some cases, first impressions might begin before you even walk through the door. One woman who used to work in personnel told me this story:

"When someone was coming in for an interview, we'd tell them to park in the lot we could see from our offices. That way, we could check out people as they got out of their cars and watch to see what they drove and how they handled themselves when they didn't think anyone was watching."

Someone else told me he would call his secretary, who had already met the person in the lobby, to get her impression on the job candidate. Then he would come out and greet the job hunter.

Now's a good time to mention the importance of *lobby etiquette*: Be pleasant and polite to receptionists. Make them your allies. This is not only because they might have input in the process, but because they can help you down the road. Later on, when you're trying to get back in touch with the interviewer, they will remember you as that "pleasant person who showed an interest in them"—they might even be willing to go out of their way for you. Treat them with respect: They are important people in this process.

Also, even though receptionists tend to say "Please have a seat," I prefer to stand while waiting in lobbies, unless the space is too small. I like to be standing when the person greets me. Standing also lets me look at art, brochures, plaques and any magazines that clue me in on the company's interests. I learn more by being mobile and aware.

First Words out of Your Mouth

Employers are also anxious to hear what you have to say. So when you answer these seemingly innocent questions, don't complain about the lack of parking, poorly marked streets or bad directions—even if it's true.

I don't care if your plane sat on the runway for an hour and then flew through two solid hours of turbulence, or if you were stopped for speeding in the car you just rented to get to the interview on time. Don't start off by complaining.

I had a client who always found something to complain about. When it was winter, she'd come in and I'd ask how she was. She'd say, "I hate driving on the freeway and having to wear so many layers of clothing."

When it was spring, she'd come in and I'd ask how she was. She'd say, "The pollen is terrible and my eyes are watering." I finally stopped asking her how she was. But she still found a way to complain.

I think she thought she was just making conversation. (I like to give people the benefit of the doubt.) But I realized she was a critical, unhappy person who I would not want around if I was an employer.

When I notice and bring up a tendency like this with a client, they usually say, "Oh, I'm not like that . . . especially in an interview."

I guess I could be the lucky one who gets to see

them as they truly are, but I don't think so. The opposite is usually the case—which is why someone is usually having a problem getting a job or getting along in his present one.

Ask people who know you how you come across or if you have any bad habits that could turn people off.

Go With the Flow

The interviewer might want to chat for a few minutes. You can initiate small talk, too. Stick with safe and positive subjects. Mention the nice write-up about the company that was in last week's paper. Bring up the artwork that you enjoyed on the walls in the lobby. Be observant.

This might be a good time to mention something you discovered in your research. "I understand you just moved your offices here . . . this is a beautiful building." You can also pick up a lot about them by how they handle this initial step.

What's on the Menu

Experienced interviewers will tell you the agenda. For example:

"First, I'd like to ask you some questions, tell you about the position and our company and answer any questions you have. We'll talk for forty-five minutes. Then, for about twenty minutes, I'd like you to meet with Alex, whose position we're looking to fill, since he's being promoted. There are a few tests we like to give, so after you meet with Alex I'll introduce you to Sharon, who will conduct those tests. That will take an hour."

Wouldn't it be nice if every interviewer did that? Don't expect it. But if they're smart, they know it will help you feel comfortable and relaxed. If the interviewer doesn't explain the process, or hasn't had a chance, be careful about taking control.

I was holding a mock interview with my client Cheryl, who's twenty-four, very enthusiastic and always intent on getting right down to business. We were practicing for her interview in Indianapolis.

Playing the interviewer, I asked, "Did you find our offices OK?"

She replied, "Yes, your map was fine and here are my references you asked for and more copies of my resumé and I also wanted to tell you about the fact that your company seems like one I would want to work for because of what I read in the information you sent and what our school placement center had to say . . ."

Don't let your exuberance or nervousness take over. Relax. Answer the question and take one step at a time. Let the interviewer set the agenda.

This rapport-setting phase usually lasts three to five minutes, sometimes longer. You'll sense when the interviewer is ready to move on. She may sit up in her chair, clear her throat, pick up your resumé or say something to change the direction of the conversation. That's when you know you're moving into Phase 2.

PHASE 2: GETTING TO KNOW YOU
Listen Up

At all times and in all phases, have your antennae (your eyes, ears and intuition) tuned in. Here's what you're looking for:

• Whether you're talking or they're talking, *watch for nonverbal clues*: signals of boredom, disapproval, doubt, confusion, interest, support and acknowledgement. Respond to these clues.

For instance, if you're talking and she looks perplexed, don't just keep going. Stop and say something like "Does that make sense?" "Did I say something that wasn't clear?" If she looks particularly interested in something you're saying, you might ask "Would you like to hear more about that?" or "Is that an issue you've dealt with too?"

• *Listen for verbal clues about problems* she deals with, areas in which she needs help and goals of the company. Take mental notes—you'll use them later.

• *Let her know what you've got.* Here is where your mental notes come in handy. Early on in your meeting an experienced interviewer will move into questions that require more than a simple yes or no answer from you. She's observing you—your expressions, your demeanor and how poised you remain. She's also evaluating your communication skills—how persuasive you are, your command of language and how you handle the entire process.

The kind of information you share also tells a lot about you. For example, let's say she starts off with: "Please tell me about yourself." You respond with:

"I'm forty-two years old and have been married to the same wonderful woman for seventeen years. We have two children who are in high school. I grew up in Pittsburgh and am very active in my church."

It's not necessarily a bad or good answer. But it may not be at all what the interviewer wants to know.

You may have also missed a great opportunity to share more relevant information about yourself that tells why you might be qualified for the job.

Some people will argue that this kind of answer demonstrates that you're a stable person. I'd prefer not to second-guess the employer. Everyone will see things differently.

A better response to this open-ended question might be: "I'd be happy to tell you about myself. Is there anything in particular you'd like to know?"

If she says, "Anything you'd like to share," stick with relevant data. This is information that supports your ability to do the job you're there to talk about.

This is when you can use parts of your three-minute commercial. (Now aren't you glad you did all that work?) Pick the highlights. Don't give examples of how you've been effective yet—that will come later. In fact, you may want to develop a shorter version that just gives an overview.

I once had an interview in which the first thing the employer asked was: "So who are you?" A three-minute commercial would have been very helpful at that point.

If she told you something about the job, or you had details in advance, see if you can relate those to what you tell her about yourself. For example, if she said they are trying to combine the bookkeeping function in this new job, you could say something like:

"I also have three years' experience in bookkeeping. When I worked for the Deevers Company, I handled everything, including accounts receivable and payables, payroll and insurance."

OTHER QUESTIONS YOU COULD HEAR:
• What is your experience in this field?
• Tell me about the business you're in now.
• Why are you leaving your current company?
• What have you been doing since the plant shut down?

- Where did you get your experience as a manager?
- How do you like this field?
- Why did you choose to be a nurse?
- What interests you about advertising?

All of these questions offer you an opportunity to let her know what you've got. Your goal is to intrigue her and get her interested in wanting to know more about you.

If you don't do this, she may start looking for ways to end the interview because she decides you're not all what she's looking for.

Stay Cool

When you're the one doing the talking, you naturally relax. So be aware that you're probably getting more comfortable as you talk. As you progress, she'll ask questions that will help her further evaluate how well you communicate, deal with stress and think on your feet. Be conversational, but don't offer information "off the record" or unsolicited.

The more she gets to know you, the more likely you'll start hearing questions such as:
- What are your strengths?
- What are your weaknesses?
- What's your greatest achievement?
- What did you like best in your last job?
- What did you like least in your last job?
- What was your relationship with your boss like?
- What interests you about our company?
- What's your leadership style?
- Tell me of a situation when you had to solve a big business problem.
- How would others describe you?

I'll talk more about responding to these questions in chapter nine.

Dig for Usable Information

This is a bit tricky. You don't want to come off as trying to control the conversation—which you're not. But you do need to snoop around for information that will help you give back information that's relevant. Here's how to do that:

The interviewer asks you questions such as: Why do you want to work here? What makes you think you can do this job? Why should I hire you? How do you think you can help our company?

If you don't know much (or anything) about the job, these are tough questions to answer. So throw the question back in his court. Say: "I'd like to share with you how I think I can contribute. It would help, though, if you could tell me more about the position, what some of the issues your department deals with are and what kinds of problems the person in this position would address."

Again, as he talks, take mental notes. Then tailor your answer accordingly.

Digging for useful information would be especially important if an actual job does not exist, but you're talking to the company to fill a potential future need.

Say What?

Don't be afraid to ask for clarification or have something repeated if you didn't understand or hear what was stated. This includes:

1. Anytime you hear a question you feel you can't answer because you need more information. Ask for it. I talked about the possibility of this in chapter five when we discussed hypothetical questions: How would you fire someone? What would you do if . . .

2. If you don't understand a question or something that was said.

You're being a good communicator if you bring these issues up. It prevents misunderstandings and enhances your rapport.

Distractions Detract

Small things can interfere with your conversation. These could be a pen that falls out of your hand while you're talking, ringing phones, a siren or a loud sound outside the window. Sometimes it's better to acknowledge them rather then pretending they didn't happen. They can be disturbing, and trying to ignore them is *another* distraction.

These little annoyances remind me of call-waiting on the telephone. If you're talking to someone and another call beeps through, out of politeness you may not say anything. But on your end, you keep hearing the beep and it distracts you from listening to the conversation you're trying to hold.

An employer told me about the time she was interviewing candidates at a job fair. She was sitting in a large room of a convention center surrounded by other people at tables who were also holding interviews. Suddenly the fire alarm went off. She definitely couldn't ignore that one. She made a joke about it, and she and the job hunter continued to talk outside.

Recognizing and clarifying things that get in the way of your discussion show that you are a skilled communicator and aren't afraid to speak up. Remember the executive recruiter who purposely made the candidate's chair sit cockeyed? His intent was to see if the job hunter would bring it up, which told him the candidate wasn't afraid to stand up for himself.

The Body Speaks

By the way, I haven't talked much about body language. Do be aware that it tells a lot about you. How you sit, eye contact and handshake are very important.

• You don't have to stare someone in the eye nonstop to have good eye contact. In fact, I had a client like that once. I didn't feel as if he was really looking at me—it was more like he was looking *through* me. When the interviewer is talking, look him in the eye and give him your full attention. Most of the time you talk, look at him. But it's natural to look away occasionally when you think and converse.

• Here's a little tip that will come in handy when you're talking to someone who either has a glass eye or one that does not look straight ahead. Pick one eye and focus on that—preferably the good eye, if you can tell which one it is.

• Even if you're not nervous, fidgeting with your fingers, clothes, glasses or hair makes you seem that way. Keep pens out of your hand, too—especially the kind that click. Everything about you, including your words, needs to communicate the same thing: I'm confident and I can do the job.

PHASE 3: GETTING TO KNOW ALL ABOUT YOU
A Picture Is Worth a Thousand Words

Remember you were cursing me back in chapter seven when I told you to write down specific examples of how you've used your strengths—what I called your "proof"? Here's the payoff.

As the interview moves along, you two will get a little cozier. The employer will dig for more specifics. He'll ask questions such as:

• What is your greatest achievement?
• How do you keep 250 distributors updated on new products?
• How have you been successful?
• Tell me about your writing skills.

Stories simplify complex issues and help people see you've got the goods by showing how you have been successful in the past. Stories also stick in their minds. So after interviewing ten people who are now one big blur, you're remembered as that guy who came up with the idea to use videos for his product introductions to distributors or the woman who saved 125 jobs by developing an innovative re-engineering plan.

No Problem

I want to remind you that at this stage—or in any of these stages, for that matter—don't bring up *your* concerns or problems. Remember those? That's right: the fact that you want a job, you want to make gazillions of dollars, you have a sick grandmother who lives with you, or your daughter needs braces or you will be needing a hernia operation sometime in the next year. Bringing these up will only muck things up.

For instance, one man I know was invited back for a second interview. Since it seemed to be getting serious, he felt he should bring up the fact that if he were to take a job with this company, he'd have to find child care for his daughter.

Why was this downright stupid to bring up? First, he hadn't been offered the position yet. Second, it had nothing to do with the company. If he wanted to work, that was an issue he needed to deal with on his own. Why bring it up? Guess what—he never got called back for another interview.

PHASE 4: DEAL WITH THE "BUTS"
Objections

"Buts," you'll recall, are interviewers' fear about your ability to do the job or fit in with the company. They must be dealt with—acknowledged and hopefully snuffed out—as you become aware of them.

The best you can do is be prepared. *Objections*, stated or implied, need to be overcome before you can move to the next phase. If they haven't been resolved, you'll probably be screened out.

PHASE 5: BRING THIS TO A SMOOTH CONCLUSION
Last Call

You know things are winding down if you hear a question like: "Is there anything else you want to share or that we need to cover?" If you haven't asked all your questions, now's your chance. And if you want to clarify a point or bring up something that didn't get covered, do it now.

If the interviewer asks if you have any questions, don't just say "No." You'll come across as disinterested. Even if all your questions are answered, either use this as the opportunity to ask about the next step, or say something like:

"You have done a good job of answering all of my questions. If I think of something when I leave, may I call you?"

Do I Detect Interest?

Something could be up when the interviewer shows you around the office, introduces you to people and asks about your availability. And of course, it's an obvious and positive sign when she brings up the fact that you should set up another interview.

But either way, find out where you stand. Get feedback and, if need be, deal with any concerns. Remember what I suggested earlier in the chapter:

"I feel very positive about everything we've discussed today. I like what your company is doing and I'm very interested in this position. Do you think my qualifications and background match what you're looking for as well as I do?"

Pay attention to what you sense—watch for hesitations that might be an unexpressed concern. If she agrees it's a good match so far, move on to the next phase.

All's Well That Ends Well

Any objections, concerns and questions should be cleared up. Now you're ready for the next phase.

PHASE 6: WHERE DO WE GO FROM HERE?
Crying, Waiting, Hoping

Don't pick yourself up and walk through that door—yet. Without some plan for the next step, you're setting yourself up for the "what ifs" and agonizing days of floating in limboland. First, you need to know what the next step is. So ask. Some suggested ways:

"Where do we go from here?"

"Since we both feel so good about this, does it make sense to set up the next interview?"

"How will you be proceeding?"

If they say they'll be interviewing more people for the next two weeks, will be back in touch or aren't willing to set up a next appointment, follow up with:

"If I haven't heard from you by such and such a date, is it OK if I call you?"

This way, you're not sitting around wondering "Why haven't I heard from them? What if they didn't like the way I answered that question about my last job? What if it was my response to their question about travel? What if . . ." You'll drive yourself and everyone crazy. I know, I've done it.

If you set up the next step, you can call them on such and such a date to find out where they are in the process. Then you can say to yourself, "I've followed up and demonstrated my interest."

But really do follow up like you say you will. Unless you have no fear of rejection, this follow-up part is hard to do. And that's the reason—people are afraid they'll be rejected. They'd rather not know. They'll say: "We had an interview, but I guess he's not interested, I've never heard back." "They never called back like they said they would." And that's the end of that. You never followed up, so you never really knew.

In 1889, Ralph Waldo Emerson said in one of his speeches, "If a man can write a better book, preach a better sermon, or make a better mousetrap than his neighbor, though he builds his house in the woods the world will make a beaten path to his door." Today, if you follow this advice when marketing yourself, you will stay alone in the woods without a job. You can have all kinds of qualifications, but you need to show your interest by following up.

I'm jumping ahead here, but when you do follow

up, if they say "We'll get back to you," again set up the next step: "When do you think you'll be making your decision? Is it OK if I check back if I haven't heard from you by next Wednesday?"

When Chris, the woman I talked about in chapter five, came back from her interview in Austin, she said, "They said they'd call me in two weeks. But they didn't call when they say they would—it's just like dating."

PHASE 7: GIVE THANKS
Verbally Thank the Interviewer and Immediately Go Home and *Type* a Thank-You Note

This is not only the courteous thing to do, but it echoes your interest and sets you apart from everyone else who probably won't send a thank-you letter. It may influence how the interviewer feels about you.

Someone once wrote to me about an interview that lasted ten minutes. He said, "The employer was rather rude and didn't seem to give a darn about me. I know I'll never get the job. Should I still send a thank-you note?"

Yes! I answered, and added that these are the kinds of circumstances that are the most difficult ones to write thank-you's for, but also the most necessary. Thank-you notes have turned bombed interviews into leads for other jobs, second interviews and job offers.

Personalize every letter. Send letters by U.S. mail—or if you want to be sure it gets there, use a delivery service that guarantees its services. (The U.S. Post Office only guarantees express mail.) Do not fax this or any other letters—unless a company specifically asks you to fax something.

Hey, I like the convenience of being able to get a piece of information to someone in California in forty-two seconds, too. But do you really know it's going to get there? I mean, once they enter Faxland, where exactly do they go anyway? They could end up in the hands of someone else and your person never gets your note. It happens—I got someone's credit report and an estimated cost from an architecture firm to rebuild an office building I didn't own. Neither of the fax numbers the information was sent to were even close to mine.

Also, odds are the person you're sending it to won't be standing there when it arrives. So someone else picks it up. Or it lands on the floor and falls behind a desk. Besides, it's just plain tacky to fax a thank-you note. Just stick it in the envelope, lick a stamp and mail it.

Incorporate specific points you discussed and remind the interviewer why you're so wonderful. Develop a format that outlines the company's objectives, areas the position would address and how you can help. It's similar to a proposal.

The sample thank-you letters on pages 82 to 84 do this.

THE HEREAFTER
Hello, It's Me

It doesn't hurt to call the interviewer back in a few days and say something like: "I just wanted to thank you again for meeting with me. I've had a couple days to think about what we talked about and want to reiterate my interest in pursuing this: Is there anything else I can do at this point? . . . I look forward to talking again."

Catching the Elusive Butterfly

What happens when you call and the person you interviewed with is in a meeting? You call back and he's on the phone. You call back and he's out of town. You get his voice mail. He doesn't return your calls. Does that mean he's not interested? There you go "what iffing" again. This thinking makes you paranoid and the next thing you know you'll be concentrating on the wrong issues. You'll begin to doubt yourself, which will affect your confidence.

Talk to the secretary and explain that you've been trying to reach Mr. Epstein. If you're very nice and explain the situation, the secretary will help track him down or tell you when he'll be available. This is why it helps if you were nice when you came in for the interview. You can also try calling your initial contact in personnel.

Sometimes people just aren't as good about getting back as you would like. I know your job search is the most important thing in the world—to you. But it does not have the same priority for everyone else. They have their own problems. People operate on what I call the Priority of the Moment.

If you're still interested in the position, continue

Jack B. Morton
1500 Lowala Lane
Maui, Hawaii 96750

March 3, 1996

Mr. Lowell Santorini
The Sylvia & Harry Company
1115 Livingston Road
Columbus, Ohio 43215

Dear Mr. Santorini:

Thank you for the opportunity to meet and discuss the position of International Sales Manager. I also appreciated you taking the time to introduce me to Mr. Darryl Williams. After talking with you both, I have a good understanding of your company's goals and feel strongly that my expertise can help you meet them.

The two areas that will require immediate attention are the establishment and training of a new sales force. I have successfully recruited, hired, trained and managed professional sales teams for two companies who were expanding into the international market. In both instances, the companies were selling products to fifteen countries and achieved record sales and earnings within one year.

I have also served on teams that examined international growth opportunities, where I proposed entry strategies that led to the opening of new manufacturing plants and joint venture relationships in the Far East.

My expertise includes development of policies and procedures to ensure consistency in service and a quality product—an important aspect of entering the international market.

I like everything I heard today about your company and this position. This is the type of challenge I thrive on and am confident I can meet, if not exceed, your goals.

I will call you on March 10 to talk further. Thank you, again.

Sincerely,

Jack B. Morton

Sample thank-you letter

Lois Marvin
1294 Main Street
Bigtown, Colorado 80302

June 11, 1996

Mr. Lee Federico
8000 Markian Way
Dallas, Texas 75229

Dear Mr. Federico:

Thank you for the opportunity to discuss the future of Miller Industries and how I can contribute to the position of Vice President of Operations and Training.

I am confident that my eighteen years of experience in this industry, in-depth knowledge of operations and training, and expertise with international markets can create the results you desire and achieve your vision for growth.

I am excited about the opportunity to be a valuable contributor to your company. Based on our conversation and my understanding of your objectives, I have outlined some of the specific ways I feel I can be of value. I will call you on June 18 to talk further.

Thank you, again.

Sincerely,

Lois Marvin

Sample thank-you letter

to show it. Send a letter. (But be nice.) Call again. Be pleasantly persistent.

Tips:
- Call when he's more likely to be in the office: early morning, midweek and mid-month.
- Have an alternate contact. See if there's someone else you can talk to.
- Make secretaries your friends.
- Ask questions: When will he be in and what's the best time to reach him?

- Leave a clear message. Explain why you called and when you'll call back.

When to Call in Your References

The simple answer is when they ask for them. When a company wants them, they'll tell you. Have them lined up and ready to go. In fact, bring a copy with you in case the interviewer asks for them.

Include the names and titles of four to six people you've worked with and worked for, their company, address and phone number.

Proposal to Miller Industries
For Position of Vice President of Operations and Training
From Lois Marvin

COMPANY OBJECTIVE

Create strategies to integrate U.S., Mexican, Canadian and new Latin American operations, resulting in more efficient use of management systems and technical resources.

HOW I WILL CONTRIBUTE

Develop and oversee implementation of training of employees on Miller Industries customer service philosophy, operational procedures and team approach that has been the cornerstone of its success.

OBJECTIVE

Lower production cost.

HOW I WILL CONTRIBUTE

• Create training programs that involve every employee and thoroughly educate them on all facets of the production process. This helps each department see how its function and contribution affect the efficient operations of our plant.

• Evaluate resources to determine personnel, equipment and new software needs.

OBJECTIVE

Better utilize production operations and distribution networks of company subsidiaries.

HOW I WILL CONTRIBUTE

Develop licensing agreements with other companies in this industry that will result in built-in promotion of company name and products and strengthen customer loyalty.

OBJECTIVE

Develop relationships with regulatory agencies and related associations to take a leadership role in changing legislation that currently hinders customer service and growth.

HOW I WILL CONTRIBUTE

Garner support of the top eight manufacturers in the industry and create and present a plan that modifies legislation and allows the company and industry the flexibility to meet customers' needs.

Sample proposal (can be included with thank-you letter)

If Worst Comes to Worst

If you do get through and he says, "We decided on someone else," it's not the end of the world. Sure you're disappointed. But for whatever reason, it just wasn't a good match. It's just the way the cookie crumbles sometimes.

See if he'll give you feedback. Don't ask: "What did I do wrong?" Instead, say: "Could you give me some feedback about how I conducted myself in the interview? . . . What you based your decision on . . . Is there something I should be aware of to strengthen my interview skills?"

If you're lucky, they'll be honest and you'll learn a good lesson—like the time I was turned down for a job with an advertising agency and I asked for input.

She said, "I didn't feel you were proud enough of your work. For one thing, the corners were dogeared on some of your newspaper ads in your portfolio. This seemed to say you didn't care enough about your work. And two, when I watched your television commercial, you played it down, pointing out what it didn't have—an elaborate budget and lots of technical jazz. I liked it, but you didn't seem to."

What could I say, except thank you for a lesson I'll never forget.

Other times, you will run into situations like the one Joanie encountered. When she asked the recruiter what kind of feedback the employer gave about her interview and why she wasn't chosen for the position, the interviewer told the recruiter, "It's not my job to critique her."

If you don't get feedback, think about what felt good and not so good about the interview. Where do you need improvement? Did you listen or interrupt when the interviewer spoke? What questions or areas did you have difficulty with? Be honest with yourself and practice with someone who will give you candid and useful feedback.

One More Angle to Consider

Is there another position you could apply for? Or is there a way to demonstrate your value somewhere else in the company . . . possibly create a job for yourself?

One of my clients did that. He was turned down for a sales position he interviewed for because he lacked experience. So he wrote the company headquarters in Atlanta, explaining that he had interviewed with their office in Ohio, what he liked about the company and what he had to offer, and then asked to be considered for the sales trainee position in another city. The day the manager got his letter, he got an interview. The manager was impressed with his determination and flew him to Atlanta— where he was offered a sales trainee position.

See, it wasn't the company that rejected him. It just wasn't a good fit for the position, or the chemistry didn't jibe with the initial interviewer.

So You Want to Be a Drop-Out

If at any point in the interview process you don't want to be considered for the position, drop out. Why would dropping out even be a consideration?

Go back to chapter one and look at the elements of The Job You Want. You're not going to get 100 percent of every single thing you want, so rate them according to importance and where you're willing to compromise. If a position doesn't meet your requirements in enough categories or the ones that matter the most, think twice about whether you want to continue the process.

If you decide it's not right for you, drop out gracefully:

"Ms. Thal, I've given this a great deal of thought and I've decided that this position isn't a good fit with my skills and goals. I like your company. I like your philosophy, your vision and focus. But I think I'd be more valuable in a different department. What I'd like to do is keep in contact and, if possible, continue to explore where I can contribute my skills to your company."

Do not make this decision too hastily, though.

One of my clients was interviewing in a city where she wanted to move and with a company she wanted to work for. The position, however, was not as challenging as she would have liked. She continued to go through the interview process anyway.

After the third interview, the company came back to her and said, "We think you're overqualified for this position, but we want to find a place for you here." They created a different position for her that was a much better fit.

What They're Up to

While you're figuring out your next step, the people who interviewed you are poring over their list of criteria that describe the ideal person for the job. They are going through the checklist and rating you accordingly. They may also be kicking around these questions:

- What was your first impression of her?
- How do you think she'd get along with Harriet and Peter?

- Do you think she's confident?
- Is her experience what we need?
- What did you think about the fact that she's changed jobs three times in seven years?

A day later, they may scrap the position you just interviewed for. Chris, who had her interview in Dallas, was called back for a third interview two months after the first one. By then, the position had completely changed and she was being considered for a different one.

You may not be privy to what's really going on. Just know that internal changes in the company, new projects or accounts the company acquires or loses, can affect what happens to you. These are all reasons they don't call you back, leaving you in limboland. But if you've always got the next step set up, it cuts down on the "what iffing" and keeps you focused on what to do next.

THE LITTLE THINGS

No matter what stage you're in, the little things matter a lot. They can enhance your image or eliminate you as a potential employee. Little things include:

Your Sunday Best

Don't wait until the morning of the interview to decide what you will wear. Make sure your suit, shirt or blouse are clean and pressed and your shoes are shined. Wear clothes you feel good in. It will affect your demeanor.

- Your clothes should fit with the decorum of the company and the position you are applying for. For white-collar positions, men should wear a conservative, tailored suit with a long-sleeved, crisp, white shirt. If applying for a blue-collar job, depending on the position and the company, a neat pair of slacks and a jacket are fine. If in doubt, wear a suit.
- Women should also wear a conservative suit. It doesn't have to be navy and you don't have to wear a plain white blouse. But nothing too froufrou, either. Neither men nor women are there to make a fashion statement. Be yourself, but be tasteful and conservative.
- Make sure there are no buttons missing on your shirt or blouse. One of my clients came to our first meeting wearing a blouse that a button had fallen off of; she had pinned it—and it showed. That

tiny little pin put an image in my head that I couldn't shake. I had the feeling that she would be sloppy or not thorough, or somehow would cut corners. Sure enough, that's exactly how she handled the assignments I gave her. She did enough to get by, but her work was always rushed, incomplete, done at the last minute and lacking depth. That one little missing button created an inconsistency in her overall look, and in my mind, a big doubt about her abilities.

- Both men and women should tone down jewelry and cologne. Men: No earrings. I know it's very hip. But so are lot of other things you'd never wear to an interview. Earrings fall into the category of scarves in your pocket or two-tone shoes; they don't belong in an interview.
- Men, make sure your socks are long enough so that when you sit or cross your legs, your bare leg doesn't show.
- What if it's Casual Day at the company when you're having your interview? It's their casual day—not yours. One of my clients had an interview in Florida at 3 P.M. When he got to his hotel around two, there was a note from the secretary of the office where he was going that said "Today is dress-down day."

He wondered if that meant he should dress down as well, or just be prepared, because the people interviewing him would be dressed casually. He wore a suit anyway. When he got there, the secretary said, "Didn't you get my note?" Her intentions were well-meaning . . . I guess. It does make you wonder, though, if the company could have set that up to see how he'd react.

Mind Your *Ps* and *Qs*

Pay attention to and practice everyday courtesies and things that you may not normally think about:

- How you act when you enter someone's office—You should wait for the interviewer to motion for you to take a seat.
- How you sit—Don't slouch, but don't look like a stiff board, either.
- Plan what you will bring—if anything. Set briefcases and portfolios next to you on the floor. Other than extra resumés, or samples of your work if appropriate, you don't need to bring anything.

Briefcases can look like a security blanket—a crutch that detracts from you. If you don't need one—which you probably don't—don't bring it.

• Don't bring your children or spouse to an interview. (Yes, I know people who have done that.) If someone is bringing you, have him drop you off and get lost. If the interviewer wants to meet your spouse, she'll let you know.

Get Me to the Interview on Time

This is so important it deserves its own section. There's no excuse for being late. None. Not even the following:

• The traffic
• The electricity went out so you didn't have an alarm
• Your car clock is broken

Scope out the location of the company the day before so you know how much time to give yourself to get there on time and park. Arrive about ten minutes early. Go to the restroom and make sure your hair is in place, your tie is straight (men) and there's no lipstick on your teeth (women).

SUMMARY

The company would like to fill a position as quickly as possible—but it probably won't happen as quickly as you would like. That's OK, because you can learn a lot as the process unfolds. It happens in stages and depends on how many people are involved, who has authority to hire, and other factors.

Sometimes, the needs of the position change or unforeseen problems crop up that are unrelated to you.

Look at the step-by-step interview process as not only a way for them to evaluate you, but as a way for you to gain insight into the company, its culture and how it fits you.

CHECKLIST

✔ Make a good first impression. You only get one chance.

✔ Listen for verbal and nonverbal clues that indicate if the interviewer likes or dislikes what she hears, is confused, supportive or wants more detail.

✔ Go with the flow. Don't try to take control.

✔ Take mental notes on what they're looking for, then let the interviewer know you've got it.

✔ Ask if you don't understand something.

✔ As the process unfolds, weigh information to decide if the position is right.

✔ Always know where you stand. Ask: Do you think this a good match?

✔ Always set up the next step. Ask: Where do we go from here?

✔ Set it up so *you* can check back.

✔ Check to see where they are in the decision-making process.

✔ Don't make hasty judgments, but do pay attention to clues on how you're treated and what their priorities seem to be.

✔ Always present yourself in the best possible light.

CHAPTER 9

Put to the Question

Strategy #9

**Anticipate the questions
and their intent, then
plan your answers.**

And now, the chapter you've been waiting for. A list of the most frequently asked interview questions and others that interviewers have been known to ask, plus questions that are none of their darn business.

What about the answers, you ask?

Having just spent eight chapters getting to know yourself, what interviewers look for, what you have to offer an employer, what to say and not say, you *have* the answers.

You could probably use some pointers on what questions to be prepared for, why the interviewer is asking the question and the kind of information that's best to share.

But pat answers—nothing doing. That defeats the whole purpose of being an unflinching, unyielding job hunter intent on getting The Job You Want. These have to be your words, your feelings and your rationale, not mine. I'm afraid I just won't be much help, because I can't be there with you in the interview. Besides you don't want to sound like you got your answers from a book.

Here, instead are:

- Subjects they could ask about
- The questions
- Insight into why they may be asking the question
- What to share and not share, along with suggested phrases (These are not necessarily to be used verbatim, but as guides to illustrate appropriate language and attitudes.)

It should be pretty easy to pluck out the data you need by the way I've organized this. I have categorized this information according to what you've determined in earlier exercises. Some questions will overlap and fit into other categories:

1. *What can you do and where have you done it?* Why do you want to do it? Why do you want to do it here? What makes you qualified? What will you do for us? How do you handle situations? I lump this together as *Skills and Work Experience.*
2. *What do you know?* How will you make a difference with what you know? How have you made a difference in the past? How will you stay current? I call this *Knowledge.*
3. *What are you like?* How do you handle situations? What are your overall style and priorities? I refer to this as *Personal Characteristics.*

Then I organized each of those categories into three areas:

A. Subjects that could come up
B. What they're looking for
C. How they might ask
   1. Information that's good to bring up
   2. Information that's not so good to bring up

Plus, I give you a technique that will help you answer many questions. What more could you ask for?

If you just graduated or are re-entering the job market, some of the questions may not apply to you.

Other questions will *only* apply to you. Even if a question doesn't sound like one you'd hear, consider how it might be reworded to apply to your situation. Here is the technique that will help you answer many of these questions.

FOLLOW THIS FORMAT TO CREATE DYNAMIC ANSWERS:

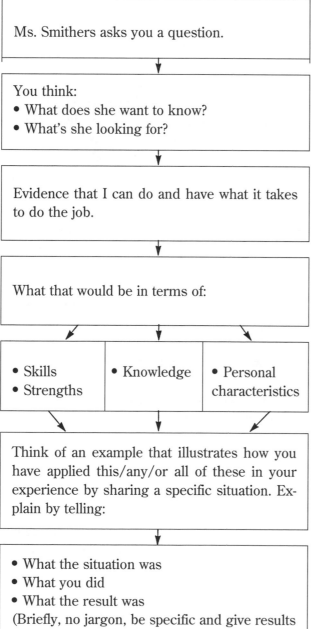

Ms. Smithers asks you a question.

You think:
• What does she want to know?
• What's she looking for?

Evidence that I can do and have what it takes to do the job.

What that would be in terms of:

• Skills • Strengths	• Knowledge	• Personal characteristics

Think of an example that illustrates how you have applied this/any/or all of these in your experience by sharing a specific situation. Explain by telling:

• What the situation was
• What you did
• What the result was
(Briefly, no jargon, be specific and give results in terms of dollars saved, relationships enhanced, quality improved, efficiency increased, sales increased, etc.)

WHAT CAN YOU DO AND WHERE HAVE YOU DONE IT? (SKILLS AND WORK EXPERIENCE)

Your skills are what allow you to make things better and more profitable for a company. So be prepared to talk about what those are, how and where you've used them (your experience) and why they've made a difference in the past.

Subjects That Could Come Up

Why you're job hunting	Accomplishments
Specific jobs	What's been rewarding
Past bosses	Disappointments
Strengths	How you've handled situations
Weaknesses	Salary
Difficulties in your career	Responsibilities

What They're Looking For

• Do you have the basic skills and qualifications to do the job?
• Can you lead people to achieve objectives? Do you recognize others for a job well done?
• What motivates you? Are you interested in more than money? In working toward a greater goal?
• How well do you get along with others, communicate, resolve conflicts and build relationships?
• How have you progressed in your career? Are you an achiever? What's important to you?
• What kind of work have you done? What is your experience?
• How productive have you been? Are you results-oriented?
• Can you define problems, implement solutions and evaluate the outcome?
• Do you take responsibility for your time, your career and your personal and professional growth?

Here are questions an interviewer could ask to find out about these things.

Tell Me About Yourself

If you decide you don't really need to prepare for any questions, promise me you'll at least prepare for this one. It's *so* common. And it's not as easy to answer as you think. Some of my most articulate clients end up rambling on and on and on if they haven't practiced.

This is asked to get the interview started, to get you talking and to find out not only what your skills and experience are, but also to get a feel for your communication skills and check you out overall.

Share the type of information discussed in chapter seven—relevant data about your career and what makes you qualified. Elements of your three-minute commercial will come in very handy here.

Veer away from giving personal information such as family, hobbies and where you grew up—unless that's what the interviewer asks for. If you're not sure what she wants, ask: "What kind of information would you like me to share?"

Here are other open-ended "icebreaker" questions that get you talking. These types of questions can establish the direction and tone of the conversation.

- **Tell me about your career.**
- **Tell me about your experience.**
- **Can you tell me about your experience since you graduated/left the Brahms Company?**
- **Tell me about your most recent position.**

Here's your chance to share:

- How long you've been in a position
- Titles you've held
- Names of companies you've worked for
- Responsibilities you've had
- How you've progressed in your career
- Professional organizations you're in
- Leadership positions you've held
- Applicable education
- Special projects you worked on
- Achievements you've accomplished in your career
- Recognitions and promotions you've received

What Do You Like About Your Job?

Other questions like this that help the interviewer delve further into the deep recesses of your mind are:

- **What kinds of problems have you faced?**
- **What are you most proud of?**
- **What do you like about your job?**
- **What are your accomplishments?**
- **Why do you like this field?**

You'll be sharing information about your strengths, what you do best and how committed you are. Hey, here's your chance to tell a story. Give lots of nice juicy particulars. Here's how:

"I'm proud of the fact that I make a tremendous difference in the lives of children and adults by helping them overcome their physical disabilities from accidents. For instance, recently I started working with a woman who was buried in the rubble of the federal building bombing in Oklahoma City. She nearly lost her left leg after being buried under glass and slabs of concrete. I am helping her undergo rigorous physical therapy, which has led to her now being able to maneuver a wheelchair and speak again."

or

"When I was in school, I completed an internship at a women's shelter. I created and implemented programs that helped homeless women find employment and housing. I organized and presented workshops that helped build these women's self-esteems and their ability to be productive citizens."

Whenever you mention an achievement or example, don't forget to use this format:

- Problem • What I did • Result

Why Did You Leave Your Company?. . . Why are you looking?

Could you promise me you'll practice this one, too? If you don't get asked this, I owe you dinner next time I'm in town. This question, in essence, is asking, "Why are you in the situation you're in?" (job hunting or unemployed). *Focus on what you want to move toward—not what you want to get away from.* Of course your answer will depend on your circumstances. But here are some ideas you can play around with:

- The company is downsizing.
- My position is being eliminated.
- I want to work for a small company.
- I want to move into a more progressive industry.

- I like what I do: however, I prefer to be in a more entrepreneurial environment.
- I'd like a position that is more hands-on.
- I want to be able to see the results of my work.
- I want to work outdoors.
- I work for a family-owned company which is run by the father and two sons and I will not have the opportunity to be a key decision-maker, so I'm looking for an opportunity in which I can contribute my talents to . . .
- I worked in sales for seven years before I left to start a family. I've been attending school this past year to update my skills and now I'm ready to work full time again.
- I just graduated college with my B.A. degree in communications and am interested in finding a position where I can apply my education and part-time work experience.

DON'T GIVE ANSWERS THAT FOCUS ON WHAT YOU WANT TO GET AWAY FROM:

- The company doesn't know what it's doing—I decided I'd better look before it's too late.
- This industry has gone to pot and I can't be without a job.
- The company I work for is so bureaucratic there's nothing to do but paperwork.
- The management doesn't appreciate me.
- The company is unethical.
- I didn't like my boss.
- My family was pressuring me to leave.
- I wasn't paid enough.
- I can't stand being at home anymore.
- I need more stimulation than I get from my four-year-old.

If you're no longer working for the company, check with your former supervisor when you develop this response. Whatever you say, it should be comfortable and compatible with what he or she would say (in the event that your answer provokes questions about why you left and the interviewer calls your former company).

What Are Your Weaknesses?

Careful. You two should be pretty cozy by now. The interviewer is banking on it—hoping you're comfortable enough to confess some personality flaw that could make you a bad choice for the position.

Share a fact that won't affect your ability to do this job or an example of something you're overcoming. Ideas:

- I was not comfortable speaking before groups, so now I'm taking a public speaking class.
- I felt at a disadvantage because I did not speak any foreign languages, so I recently enrolled in Spanish classes.
- I'm not mechanically inclined (as long as your job does not require that you be so inclined).

How Do You Stay Current?

That's pretty straightforward. Tell her about professional journals you read, as well as classes and training you have taken.

What Are Your Strengths?

You know these if you did your homework in chapter one.

Remember: These are a few of your favorite things—what you enjoy doing most. When you enjoy doing them, you're happier, more productive and more valuable. The company wants to best utilize these talents.

What Don't You Like in Your Job?

Tempted to throw caution to the wind on this one? Don't. Don't volunteer subjects that take jabs at the company or stir up a hornet's nest, such as: people who can't communicate . . . people who never listen the first time . . . when I have to repeat myself five times . . . customers who return things . . . when management lies.

Stick to examples such as:

- The fact that we had to eliminate fifty jobs this past year.
- There wasn't anything I disliked except the fact that my job was eliminated.
- Although I know it's a part of my job, I'm not fond of paperwork. Of course, it's important and our projects won't be completed on time without the necessary paperwork, so I always get it done.
- There really isn't anything I dislike, but I do

enjoy the daily contact with our customers the most.

What Are Your Qualifications?

Time out. You need more data before you can answer this. Is she asking for your academic or job experience? Ask. Assuming it's related to your job, make sure you know what the job calls for before you answer.

If you don't know much about the job, say: "Could you tell me more about the position so that I can directly relate my qualifications?" Then give examples of skills and projects that relate to the position, always ending with—what? That's right—the results.

How Long Would It Take You to Be Productive?

You don't need to portray yourself as Superman or Superwoman by saying "Immediately." Be realistic. First you need to know the expectations of the job to answer this.

Ask what she thinks your initial responsibilities might entail. Address that, depending on what she says, or say something like: "If there is a project that needs attention right away, I have the experience and background to be productive immediately."

But also add: "I've always found I'm more effective as time goes on, as I get to know the people and the internal processes in a new job. So I'd anticipate a few weeks of getting oriented."

Where Do You Want to Be in Five Years? . . . What Are Your Long-Term/Short-Term Goals?

Short-term goals deal with getting the right position for now. So talk about that.

Long-term goals can include where you want to be with this company in the future or where you see yourself headed in the profession. Share desires such as being a key decision-maker in the organization, having significant impact on the international growth of the company or other things the interviewer has mentioned as areas of opportunity and focus.

If, let's say, you're interviewing as a manager for a restaurant, here's a sure-fire way to never hear from that company again. The interviewer asks what your long-term goals are and you say: "I want to start my own restaurant." This implies: "Teach me everything you know so I can leave you and go out and start my own thing and compete with you."

What Kind of Salary Are You Looking For?

Doesn't it seem a bit premature to talk about salary at this point? That's exactly what you tell the interviewer. Tell him you're more interested in hearing about the job, the responsibilities and whether it's a good match.

Then ask for more information about the job. I give much more detail in chapter ten, where I talk about salary negotiations. Promise me you'll work on this one, too.

How Long Would You Stay?

The interviewer wants to know just how committed you are. Are you just here for the great benefits? To learn new skills? Or do you really care about what's best for the company?

Tell her that you would plan to be in the position as long as you both feel you're being productive, you're growing and making a valuable contribution. It's true, isn't it?

What Kinds of People Do You Like to Work With?

Think about it and create your own list. If you're stuck, here are some suggestions: people who are team players, honest, caring, self-starters, motivated, creative problem-solvers, people I can learn from and people who have integrity.

What Kinds of People Do You Find Difficult to Work With?

Again, think about it and create a list that *adds* to your credibility. These could be clock-watchers, people who are late, who complain a lot and don't offer solutions, or people who don't care about meeting deadlines.

What Would You Do If You Didn't Get Along With a Co-Worker?

What a great time to tell another story—like the time you turned around a bad situation. Here, let me jog your imagination:

"Once I was on a temporary assignment for about a month. My co-worker on the project—who I had never worked with before—had the same goals in completing the assignment, but she handled things very differently than me. She was accustomed to doing things on her own and didn't seem to want any input from me. There was a lot of tension.

"First, I reminded myself that everyone's approach is different and that there's nothing wrong with her. Then I decided to use this as an opportunity to brush up on my interpersonal skills. One morning, I said to her, 'I sense there's some tension here.' What a difference that one comment made! She spilled out everything on her mind. I listened and asked her how she thought we could work together better. We not only reached our mutual goal but, from that point on, had a mutual understanding. We're good friends today."

How Do You Like Your Present Manager/Boss?

Wow, somebody actually wants to hear you complain? Your friends are sick of hearing about it—so is this your big chance to get it all off your chest? You do that, and you're out of there faster than you can say "Exit, stage left."

The only response I'd give is neutral information, such as:

- The person I report to in my present position is the Vice President of Operations.
- He's very experienced in the retail business.
- He's taught me a lot about mass merchandising, customer service and marketing.
- Since he's in Washington, I only see him twice a month.
- We have a good working relationship.

Big no-no's are judgmental commentary such as:

- He's the *best* boss I've ever had.
- He's the *worst* boss I've ever had.
- Anything in between.

(See chapter six for a lot more detail.)

What Made You Choose This Field?

If you're just out of school, looking for a new job in the same field or making a career change, here are some feasible answers:

- Your early interest in the field, people who influenced you
- Your natural talents to do the job
- Your research indicates it's a good fit with your skills and interests
- Your early experiences in a related field
- It was a natural progression based on your experience in . . .

Don't give information that makes you sound disinterested or uncommitted, such as:

- I don't know what else to do.
- My mother said I should do it.
- It pays well.
- My father was a lawyer, so I figured, why not?
- My career counselor at school said it was secure . . . and that I'd be good at it.

Isn't This a Career Change?

You too would have some question lurking in your mind if you were interviewing somebody who had been a building contractor and now wanted to be an advertising account executive. The interviewer's big concern is that you have the skills, knowledge and attitude to do the job.

Give reassurance that:

1. It's not a total flip-flop; you've done the same kinds of things before or have the necessary skills and knowledge. Let's use this true example of a person who was a contractor and wanted to be an advertising account executive:

"Having had my own business as a contractor, I met with potential customers, asked questions about their needs, developed estimates and sold them on my ability to do the job. Then I would supervise the work, bringing together people with specialized areas of expertise and getting them to complete the project to the customer's satisfaction on time and within budget.

"In the advertising business, I'd be meeting with clients, asking questions about their needs and problems, developing estimates and selling them on my ability to handle their business. Then I'd oversee the work, again by bringing together people with different areas of expertise and completing the project on time, within budget and to the customer's satisfaction. So I do have the necessary skills."

2. You have the necessary knowledge:

"From my recent education and internship, I understand the direct-mail business, how brochures and ads are produced and the printing process. I also have been very involved in politics, having developed strategies and coordinated campaigns for two ballot issues and several congressional candidates. So I have a thorough knowledge of how to develop marketing strategies and put them into action. And I'm using the same skills, just in a different environment."

Don't slip in a teensy-weensy bit of uncertainty or doubt about your ability to do the job. Sure you'll be nervous about trying something new. But you have to completely believe in your ability if you're going to convince someone else.

Even if you've been a puppet, a pauper, a pirate and a poet, look for some way to tie it all together or explain how the skills you used are transferable.

What Do You Find Difficult to Do?

Here's a good time to display your incredible problem-solving abilities, above-average intelligence, astonishing resourcefulness and concern for the company. Tell about something that was a problem and made your job or experiences difficult. Example:

"When I took this job as editor of publications, one of my responsibilities was to incorporate company news from all twelve divisions around the country. This was difficult unless I visited the region, which was cost-prohibitive. So I put out a call for division reporters who would have the responsibility of digging up news and writing stories for the newsletter. The response was tremendous. I have more news than I can use, morale has increased significantly and there's much more of a team effort."

or

"In my senior year, I was in charge of motivating a group of students in our fraternity to give up their Saturday evening for three weeks and be involved in raising money for our Association for the Blind. I set up a system where volunteers got points that went toward their chores. It worked like a charm and we raised $4,500."

Share something that used to be a problem for you, but you overcame it. For example:

"I used to be petrified of speaking in front of a group. I realized that in order to grow professionally, I would need to overcome that. So I enrolled in the Dale Carnegie public speaking class and I enjoyed it so much, I started a Toastmasters chapter in our company."

Why Were You Fired? . . . Why Didn't You Get Along?

Nobody wants to hire a problem, so don't paint that picture. Sometimes people get in jobs they're not cut out for. Most interviewers will understand if you explain without accusing or whining. Think through your situation and respond with artfully chosen words. Say things such as:

• I'm a very energetic person and my position required me to sit at a computer all day. The job was just not suitable for me and the company and I both decided it just wasn't a good match.

• I enjoyed the work I did but didn't feel comfortable in such a large organization. I decided that I'd be much happier in a small firm.

• My talents are in dealing with people. When I took the position, I was in sales for six months. Then a new manager came in and changed my job to sitting behind a desk all day working with numbers. I wasn't using my best skills. I became unhappy and it was evident, so the new manager asked me to leave. I should have done something about it before it got to that point, but I had hoped things would change.

• There was a very specific set of circumstances that led to my leaving. I was with the Fox Company for eight years. It was a good experience. Unfortunately, the company requested I make two more moves out of town. Even though they offered me a promotion, I didn't feel either move would be in the best interest of my family. I had already moved six times in those eight years.

Some situations are very touchy and need to really be thought through. Attitudes and personality traits are usually what put jobs in jeopardy. These include:

• Arrogance and aggressiveness—someone who thinks he deserves special privileges or boasts

• Chronic absenteeism and tardiness

- Not following instructions and ignoring company policies
- Complaining
- Taking credit for others' work
- Lack of enthusiasm for your job and the company
- Goofing off and taking care of personal business on company time
- Dishonesty and lying

If personalities or improper handling of situations were reasons for your departure, put a lot of thought into the wording of this answer. Example:

Paul was accused of padding his expense reports and was fired. He had been promoted three times and everything was fine until a new manager came in. He felt he had been treated wrongly and that the whole thing was a misunderstanding.

He needed a short explanation that didn't get into the gory details. Something like:

"I was with B.J.'s for nine years. I was very successful, received a number of promotions and outstanding performance reviews. I had every reason to believe I was in a strong position with the company. Someone misunderstood an expense voucher and wrongly accused me of padding an expense check. It wasn't true and unfortunately I was not given a chance to defend myself."

Don't make negative comments about the company, such as:

- The company didn't appreciate me . . . never listened to me . . . was stupid enough to let our entire department go.
- Stay away from the word "fired"—it's too emotional. Instead, use "severed relations," "mutually agreed to part ways," or "a set of circumstances that led to my leaving."

Why Have You Been Out of a Job So Long?

Whoa. Who said you have been? This is a negatively stated question that you don't want to fall for.

Tell the interviewer that you don't feel you've been out of a job so long, then prove that you have not just been sitting there watching time go by. Tell about the productive ways you're spending your time and the research you've been conducting to make sure your next position is a good match for everyone.

You'll hang yourself by giving negative information or having a "sour grapes" attitude by saying, "It's just a lousy job market and nobody wants an overqualified, fifty-year-old engineer." See chapter six for more details.

What Regrets or Disappointments Do You Have?

Now you're going to demonstrate how realistic and mature you are. Show him you're someone who focuses on the here and now, not the then and there.

Try something like:

"I've learned from all my experiences . . . besides, you can't change the past."

If you choose to share anything specific, do it like this:

"I decided to leave college my last year and have a family. I certainly don't regret having done that, but I had always wanted to complete my degree. So last year I went back to school and finished my course work and got my degree in marketing."

Definitely don't tell about poor decisions you've made, bad job choices or, as one person said, his first marriage.

How Would You Handle . . . .

an angry customer . . . a problem employee . . . What did you do when . . . What about the time when . . . How would you increase sales . . . improve morale . . . keep us competitive . . . ?

I call these behavioral and hypothetical probes (discussed in chapter four), "Show Me" questions. The interviewer wants you to show him how you'd act in the situation he portrays.

To answer these questions, you may need more information. Or you can say that how you'd react would depend on the circumstances. Then you can give an example of a similar situation that did happen, explaining how you handled it and the results of how this made the situation or company better. For example, you are asked how you would handle employee theft:

"I had to deal with that problem where I work now. I supervise thirty employees and petty theft was rampant—everything from postal stamps and office supplies to cheating on expense vouchers, padding travel reimbursements and making personal long-distance phone calls. No corporate policy existed. I would not tolerate it at any level. So first I talked to personnel to make sure there was not already a policy in existence. Then I talked to management about the best way to handle it. I gave my suggestions, which included holding a meeting with my employees to express my stance on the issue— that theft would not be tolerated and people who were found guilty would be terminated. I also suggested that, since I suspected someone in particular, I hold a meeting with him.

"I did both, and when I held my meeting with the individual, I was careful not to accuse. I told him it had been brought to my attention that he had made dozens of personal long-distance phone calls. We completely turned around the problem within two months."

. . . or if they say:

"People tend to have a lot of meetings here, which can waste a lot of time. How would you make sure a meeting was necessary?" You could say:

"I agree, sometimes meetings can waste time. So I ask that exact question that you posed: When someone wants to meet, I ask, 'Is this meeting necessary?' Many times you can accomplish the same thing by using the phone, writing a memo, using e-mail or just dropping by someone's office. That question gets people thinking about it. When only a meeting will do, I make them productive by setting goals in advance and putting them in writing, sending out an agenda the day before the meeting, asking for their input and, at the end, getting clear on who will do what next."

WHAT DO YOU KNOW? (KNOWLEDGE)

You have gained a body of knowledge and expertise after working on certain tasks, in a particular field or completing an education. Writing this out in chapter one forced you to think about the depth of what you know—capabilities and expertise you might take for granted.

Subjects That Could Come Up
- Education and training
- Technical aspects of the job
- Accomplishments

What They're Looking For
- Do you have the knowledge and expertise to do the job?
- What type of contribution will you make? What level of knowledge and accomplishment do you have?
- Is your training relevant for this job?
- How much do you know about the technical aspects of this job? What is the depth of your knowledge?
- How willing have you been to stay updated in this field?
- How current are you?
- How interested are you in this field?
- What do you expect to get from this job?

Here are questions an interviewer might ask to find out about the things I just listed.

Tell Me About Your Education

Give relevant information that supports your work. Start with your highest degree. Include:

- Your degrees
- Course work you've taken or subjects you studied
- Continuing education classes you've taken
- Where you went to school

Are you tempted to bring up what you *don't* have? This detracts from your marketability. For example, if you don't have a degree, don't dwell on it. Don't even bring it up. If they do, acknowledge it, but add:

"I did attend evening classes for two years (or whatever education you do have), and (if true) I plan to continue working toward my degree. I do feel, though, that my ten years of experience in bookkeeping have equipped me with the firsthand knowledge of how to do this job efficiently and effectively."

If you're concerned about your age, don't bring up your year of graduation from college. And especially if you're concerned about your age, don't mention your year of graduation from high school. In most circumstances, it's irrelevant anyway.

How Do You Stay Updated in Your Field?

This is another straightforward response you can give by sharing an overview of the kinds of courses you've taken to stay current, to learn new skills or expand your knowledge. If there are too many to list, give the general categories such as leadership, computers, diversity, change management.

If you're talking with a peer or direct manager, he may want to hear about the specific courses and what you learned.

But this is also a way to illustrate what kind of person you are. For example, a physics college professor attended the university's Summer Learning Institute on Instructional Technology to learn how to use software that creates images on a screen to animate lectures and enhance the learning of his two hundred-student classes.

Now here's a great opportunity for him to show how he is willing to change from plain old outdated lectures of regurgitating facts and learn new technology to improve his teaching.

If you've worked for a large company and have taken many courses, get a list from personnel. Just make sure you refresh your memory on courses you've taken. It's easy to forget.

Some courses may not be related to your field or company-sponsored—such as foreign language or computer classes. Distinguish between those related and not related by saying:

"Courses I've taken to enhance my knowledge in health care include . . . I also felt I would be more well-rounded and up-to-date with today's technology if I knew how to create spreadsheets, so I'm taking a course in that at our community college."

What Books and Publications Do You Read?

Assume this question is asking for business-related reading materials. Ask if you're not sure. List the professional journals and trade publications applicable to your field and news magazines and newspapers such as *The Wall Street Journal*, *Fortune* and *U.S. News and World Report*.

What Have You Learned . . .
from your jobs . . . from managing your home . . . from your education?

Here's a great time to display your understanding of how personal skills, leadership, attitude, being organized, self-discipline and the ability to work with others are as important as the technical skills and knowledge necessary to be successful in your work.

Other ideas you can incorporate are:

- How important it is to listen to people
- How the field you're in has changed and the ways you or the business has adapted
- An example of how you've applied your knowledge and these other skills in your particular work setting, at home or in a school or volunteer project
- How important it is to acknowledge and celebrate each person's contribution

Example:

"I started a 'Caught Me' pin program. Whenever someone caught another employee doing something right, doing a good job or even something small but significant, the employee told management and the person got a 'Caught Me' pin."

How Did You Handle . . .
What did you do when . . . What problems have you run into when . . . ?

All of these questions are looking for your breadth of knowledge, examples of how you have applied your knowledge and your level of expertise. Spell out examples, using the format of explaining the situation, telling what you did and the result.

What Kinds of Projects Did You Work on at the Figment Company? . . . Tell Me About Projects That Demonstrate Your Highest Level of Achievement

These are more straightforward questions that give you the chance to share more of your spellbinding achievements, such as:

"I am in charge of developing diversity training programs for our company." Then give an example:

"For example, I just developed a new program for our staff and trained all of the management on multicultural issues in the workplace. The program has become the benchmark for diversity training in several companies across the United States."

or

"In a volunteer capacity I headed the publicity committee for the Ensemble Theatre Group since its inception four years ago. It's now nationally recognized for its innovative productions."

or

"When I was in school I was in charge of increasing the dwindling corporate donations of the Friends of New York nonprofit organization. I recruited volunteers to initiate a direct-mail and phone campaign that resulted in a 50 percent increase in local corporate gifts."

How Will You Make a Difference in Our Company?

Obviously, to answer this question you need to know the problems of the company. If you don't know, ask. Once you know, share how you've solved similar problems in the past. Remember, that's why they're hiring you: to make things better than they are now. Here are examples:

"Based upon your company's interest in expanding into international markets, I bring to the table fourteen years experience in new market development, with eight of those years in developing European and Latin American markets. An example of how I made a crucial difference in my present company is . . ."

or

"The aerospace industry had been having problems with corrosion. I oversaw the study of the effects of corrosion on various materials and protective coatings. The results were incorporated into a computer program that is used throughout the aerospace industry today. I can help your company with similar problems."

How Does Your Work Contribute to the Overall Goals of the Company?

This is another one of those opportunities to give an example that ends in a fascinating result:

"Our management's goal was to reduce sexual harassment claims by 90 percent over two years. The training programs I developed have been credited for reducing those claims by 90 percent in the first year they were implemented."

Why Are You Interested in Working Here?

You will put the interviewer to sleep if you answer the way 99.9 percent of the jobhunters do:

"I'm looking for an opportunity where I can be challenged and advance." Companies are not there to give you an opportunity to be challenged and advance. You knew that, but you were still tempted to give that answer, weren't you? Instead, try this much more effective two-part answer:

1. What you liked based on what you learned about the company. Remember all the research you'll do, which we discussed in chapter four?
2. How you can contribute based on what you know they're looking for. Obviously, to tell that, you need to know what they're looking for in terms of skills and experience.

Example:

Part 1: "I'm impressed with what I've learned about your company—that you're the world leader in the manufacturing of widgets. Also, in talking with other employees here and based on my research, your values seem to be in line with mine. For instance, the article in last week's paper talked about your commitment to customer service. I think that is key to the future of widget companies . . . when I was with the Avi Company, I developed a customer service program that . . ." End with the impact of your contribution.

Part 2: "Based on what I know about this position, you're looking for someone with my qualifications and skills, someone who can: manage the daily operations of a widget production line, conduct training, work well in a team environment, take initiative, create a cohesive, productive staff, and someone who is experienced in customer service."

WHAT ARE YOU LIKE? (PERSONAL CHARACTERISTICS)

Your personal characteristics and attitudes show how you do things, ways that you apply yourself and your willingness to do what it takes to be successful. Each company determines what kinds of personal characteristics are important for its organization and the job.

Subjects That Could Come Up

Stressful situations	Books you read
Hobbies	Organizations you
Successes	belong to
Disappointments	Overtime and travel

What They're Looking For

How well do you handle stress?	What's your management style?

How well do you manage time?

Are you decisive, mature, socially astute?

Do you have good judgment?

Are you dependable, flexible, honest, a team player, a leader?

What's your energy level?

Do we have good chemistry?

Are you determined dedicated, confident, poised?

Are you organized?

Do you have initiative?

The interviewer looks for clues about personal characteristics by listening to your answers to all types of questions and watching body language. The following questions could be specifically asked to find out more about the type of information I just listed.

How Would You Describe Yourself?

This should sound familiar by now. Remember your personal qualities and characteristics you listed in chapter one? That's one place that will get you thinking. If you're not sure, ask people who know you how they would describe you.

What Has Made You Successful in Your Life?

I think this is a great question to think through whether or not you ever hear it. The information you come up with will help you learn things about yourself you may not have ever considered. Here's why.

I find that there are certain characteristics, interests and personality traits, evident throughout people's entire lives, that create patterns of success. Many times they are relevant to our careers. After you've given this some thought, you may be able to come up with an answer like this:

"I have always been an empathetic person, very dedicated to anything I did and mature for my age. For instance, ever since I was young, I enjoyed visiting my relatives in nursing homes, taking care of my younger brothers and sisters and the neighbor children. As a teenager, I volunteered as a Candy Striper at the hospital and for Meals On Wheels. I think this has helped me be a compassionate health care professional and also understand the personal and emotional needs of people."

or

"I have always been a leader in classes, groups I belong to and throughout my professional career. I was president of our college sorority, captain of the basketball team in high school, organized food drives for several school organizations and continue to be active in community affairs as president of the Downtown Development Committee and our company's Minority Development Board."

or

"I have always enjoyed teaching. For example, my freshman year I tutored adults and refugees to prepare for the GED, giving them educational credentials to obtain employment."

What's Important to You?

That could mean anything, so this is one of those questions that requires more data. Ask: "Can you be more specific . . . do you mean in terms of personal values . . . in a job . . . ?"

If she's looking for personal values or what you want in a job, look back at your list in chapter one. The only thing not to mention from that list is the salary.

What Do You Do When You're Not at Work? . . . What Are Your Hobbies?

Interviewers like to know what you do on those sweet Sundays with nothing to do as well as other days of the week. This is your opportunity to paint a picture of the well-rounded, balanced individual that you are. Name professional or community groups you belong to, hobbies, books you read, volunteer activities you're involved in, classes you're taking and sports you play.

Do, though, think about the potential impact of what you share. For example, do you want an interviewer to know your religious affiliation or political views? Of course it shouldn't matter, but this is not a perfect world, so it just might influence the interviewer.

So I wouldn't share potentially controversial organizations or groups that indicate political views unless applicable to the job. For example, if you are interviewing for a job with a conservative think tank in Washington, it makes sense to share the fact that you've been a member of the Young Republicans since you were twenty-one.

An African-American client of mine wanted interviewers to know about his membership in a black fraternity, for example, because he was targeting minority-owned companies.

On the other hand, you might feel that you want the interviewer to know exactly who you are even if it has no relevance to the job. One of my clients felt strongly about volunteering information about groups that indicated her religion, because, as she put it, "I want them to know who I am and what I'm about."

If you ask me, I think this is irrelevant to whether you're qualified for the job—which is what you want to be concentrating on until you get an offer. The reason they asked about outside interests is to gain insight into your personality, what kind of person you are and if you have balance in your life (unless they are truly prejudiced). These are issues that could affect what kind of employee you would make.

How Do You Feel About Working Evenings or Overtime?

You want to give an answer that demonstrates your willingness to do what it takes to get the job done, your understanding that deadlines and important projects require additional work . . . *but* you also have a life outside of work. To make both of these points, use phrases such as:

- I am dedicated to doing the best possible job . . .
- This kind of work or position requires a flexible schedule and willingness to do what it takes to get the job done . . . I've always done that . . .
- But, it's also important for me to incorporate other activities that are important to me, such as my family . . . friends . . . regular exercise program . . . so I do expect balance.
- But in order for me to be productive in my work, I do need balance.

How Do You Feel About Travel?

My first response to this question is: "Does this job require a lot of travel?"

If you're dead set against a single day out of town, now is the time to deal with it. If the job requires it and you're not willing to do it, why waste any more time discussing the position?

On the other hand, if travel isn't an issue, say it's no problem.

What's Your Leadership Style?

Don't confuse leadership with management. When asked about leadership you can explain:

- How you help others achieve goals and objectives.
- How you recognize people.
- How you evaluate people.
- How you inspire and influence others.

If you're not sure how to answer this and what these issues really mean, bone up on your knowledge. Read books on leadership. If you're going to make it in today's workforce, you need to understand this. (See chapter two.)

How Would Others Describe You?

This is another place where some of the personal characteristics you listed in chapter one come in nice and handy.

How Would You Deal With a Situation in Which a Decision Had to Be Made But There Was No Procedure for Dealing With It?

She's looking for your ability to problem solve and make decisions, as well as your dedication to the company. Here's how you can show her you're all that and more:

"Assuming my manager was not available and the situation was urgent, I would use my best judgment in making a decision about what to do. Then I would either write my boss a memo or tell her what happened."

If you can think of a situation in which something like this really happened, share that.

What Do You Spend Most of Your Time Doing and Why? . . . Describe a Typical Day in Your Work

Call attention to how you prioritize and manage your day to accomplish your goals and what those goals might be. Effective use of time is very important. Example:

"The next day starts for me at the end of the previous one, when I go through my calendar or "to do" list, check off what I've accomplished, note what didn't get done and plan my projects for the next day. Typically, I do my writing in the morning when the office is quieter. I schedule meetings with clients on Tuesdays, Wednesdays and Fridays when their schedules seem to be the most flexible."

You can also include time-savers you use:

"I always check, then double-check my work. I subscribe to the philosophy: 'If you're going to do something, do it right.' "

"When I'm done with my work, I give it to my assistant to review. She provides an objective perspective that I value highly. Sometimes she sees details that I've overlooked, that if not caught, could have caused problems. I surround myself with and depend on good people."

What's Made You Successful in This Profession?

Let the interviewer know what makes you tick. Give some characteristics that are important to the type of work you do. Example:

"This kind of work requires great attention to detail and a lot of follow up; an understanding and commitment that I am ultimately responsible for what happens; willingness to be open with my team members and a lot of support from the people I work with."

If You Had the Freedom to Be Anything, What Would it Be?

Hey, this is a free country, isn't it? So what's the deal with this question? Well, since you do have the freedom to be anything, that's why you're here at this interview. In other words, you want to be in the job you're interviewing for. Describe it. Don't say:

"I'd like to be a poet . . . a dancer . . . a public speaker . . . an astronaut" or something that has nothing to do with the job for which you're interviewing. As the interviewer, I'd wonder why you aren't doing what you really want to do and question your commitment to *this* job.

Stranger Questions

Although not as common, these are questions interviewers have been known to ask. I admit, some are pretty strange. You may never hear a single one. They all seem to be after one thing—insight into your personality. If you do hear these, or ones like them, remember there are no right or wrong answers. No matter how strange the question seems, look for a way to disclose something positive about yourself. Look them over, read what might be behind the question and be prepared for anything.

ON A SCALE OF ONE TO TEN, HOW DO YOU RATE YOURSELF—ONE BEING MEEK, TEN BEING AGGRESSIVE?

Actually this was a pretty good question for the person who got it. My client was applying for a job that required her to be fairly assertive, decisive and to feel comfortable asking questions and giving feedback in situations where she didn't know the people. A meek person would not feel comfortable or do well in that job.

WHO ARE YOUR HEROES?

Mmmm, hadn't thought about that one, had you? Depending on how you answer it, you'll give clues about your personality, style, values and interests—even your morality.

For example, if your heroes are William Shakespeare, Thomas Jefferson and Ludwig van Beethoven, I'd probably conclude:

- You enjoy art and philosophy.
- You're a thinker and are driven by personal convictions and beliefs.
- You place value on the human spirit.

IF YOU WERE TO DESCRIBE YOURSELF AS A CAR, WHAT KIND WOULD YOU BE? OR WHAT KIND OF ANIMAL WOULD YOU DESCRIBE YOURSELF AS?

You have to think about that one, too. This could be probing for how you interpret things, your creativity and abstract thinking, or how you see yourself. A Mercedes Benz, for example, says status and ego. Do you think a golden retriever means you're friendly, eager to please and loyal?

ARE YOU INTERESTED IN SPORTS?

The interviewer is probably wondering how much experience you've had working on a team and getting along with others, or if you're competitive. If you're like me—not interested in sports—you need to acknowledge the importance of being a team player, getting along with others in a job and how you always give 100 percent. If you do like sports, tell about your involvement.

You can also give examples of other ways that you work as a team member. I have told about the plays and musical productions I've been in, committees I sit on and group projects I'm involved in.

Just remember that employers hire and promote people who can work well in groups and who bring a spirit of enthusiasm to the group. They're relying more on collaborative efforts these days, so more emphasis is placed on teamwork.

How to Prepare for Any Question

• Learn your three-minute commercial.

• Think through the kinds of problems you would face in this position and be ready to give examples of how you have done that in the past.

• Go through every one of the questions I just listed and outline how you would respond.

• Always take the high road and end on a positive note—even if you're describing a problem or dealing with a concern. For example, if the interviewer said something about your lack of education, acknowledge it: "That's correct, I do only have two years of college." But don't stop there. Add: "I do feel that my six years working in operations have given me an invaluable education, which has prepared me for the challenges I'd face in this position."

• Record yourself on video (at least on a tape recorder) so you can hear your words, inflections and attitude. If you see yourself, you can check out your nonverbal communications.

• Practice with someone. After you've given a response, ask how the person felt about your answer. If you find yourself getting defensive, remember that this person is trying to help you. If he or she felt your answer was brusque, odds are your interviewer will think the same thing.

The Graduate

If you just graduated from school, you need to consider a few things:

• Your degree does not guarantee you a job.

One of my just-out-of-college clients was frustrated when I, acting as an employer, asked, "Why should I hire you?" to which he replied, "Because I have a degree in marketing," and I responded with "So what?"

I've had many clients who had masters and doctorates who were waiting tables. You will need to show employers that you have a lot more than a degree going for you.

• Most employers don't care if you received an *A* in every course you took.

• Employers know you're not going to have a wealth of experience.

• Employers don't expect you to have an in-depth understanding of the world of business. But I've noticed one thing about many people just out of school: They don't know *anything* about the world of business.

Find out what kinds of businesses exist, what they do and why they do it and why you would be doing the job you're trying to get. Don't gloss over this advice. Let me say that again. Know *why* you would do the job you want to do. It's not enough to be able to do a job; you need to understand why you're doing it. This will help you identify with employers' needs and explain how you will help them.

Before you go to any interview, write out this question:

Why would I do this job? (No, it's not to keep your parents out of your hair, buy a car or move into your own apartment.) *In other words, how does your contribution help the company?* Then answer it.

Talk to people who are in business and find out what they do. Talk to your parents' friends, neighbors and professors and ask questions. What's a typical day like? How do they like this business? Would they recommend it to a young person? Why or why not?

The Fundamental Things of Life

Employers would, however, like to see that you:

1. Have the ability to problem solve, adapt and learn quickly. They'll observe your overall communications and the way you handle yourself to get a read on that.

2. Have the ability to think on your feet. One employer told me he asks, "What have you done in the past to think on your feet?" Responses have included "Can I think about it and get back to you?"

This answer hardly demonstrates that ability.

3. Are a leader. You demonstrate this with involvement in or being an officer for a group in school or community organizations.

4. Set goals. Summer jobs with Fortune 500 companies or other business firms tell employers that you have some type of career plan—more so than someone who had waiter or waitress jobs.

5. Have the ability to clearly communicate. No "And I'm like . . ." and "He goes . . ." (See chapter seven—please.)

6. Have realistic salary expectations. Employers will be turned off if, when they ask you about salary, you say, "I need *X* amount of dollars because I'm still paying my school loans." That's a "what can you do for me" response.

Instead, you'll want to share that you feel you bring a fresh perspective and knowledge about the latest techniques in this field (and whatever else you can add) and therefore much value . . . and that you're open to discussing salary when you both decide it's a good match.

Be prepared to demonstrate or give examples of everything you say you can do. If you say you want to get into marketing, know why. Be able to describe the skills it requires and give examples of how you've used those skills in your school, community or summer jobs.

Other Situations People Worry About

WHAT IF YOU'RE ASKED A QUESTION ON SOMETHING YOU DON'T KNOW ABOUT?

Sarah, a human resource professional, told me about her interview with the director of compensation for an international company where this happened.

"He asked, 'What do you know about compensation?' I replied, 'Very little.' He told me that during an interview, you shouldn't say you don't know an answer. But I wasn't going to try to bluff someone who oversees compensation for the entire company. I told him that. He said he found my answer honest and refreshing, but destructive."

I think the best approach lies somewhere in between. First, always be on the up and up if you don't know something. But embellish your answer with more than just "very little" or a response that sounds curt. Try something like:

"My human resource expertise has focused on training and development. I have had some exposure in the area of compensation, but it is limited. However, it is an area I'd be interested in knowing more about. Does this position involve work in the compensation area?"

HOW DO YOU FIND OUT WHAT REALLY HAPPENED TO THE LAST PERSON IN THIS POSITION?

One of my clients, who was interviewing for a training position in a computer company, called to say: "I heard they just let someone go on a whim and I'm afraid they'll do that to me. I knew the person who was fired—she was doing a great job."

First, what you hear may not be the whole story. So be wary of taking sides.

Second, that situation is none of your business. I'd be cautious about bringing it up. It only affects you if the person who was terminated was your boss, because then you wouldn't know who to report to.

It's OK to ask why the position is open—and that's how I'd ask. Don't say, "I heard you fired Francis. What happened?"

If he makes reference to the situation, look for clues. Does he seem uncomfortable about it? Does he offer an explanation? How does he seem to feel about what happened?

If the person fired would have been your manager, once you're talking seriously about a job there, you can say: "Who would I be reporting to?"

Definitely don't hint that you're afraid you might be axed at his whim. You'll find out more by asking appropriate questions, such as: What are the expectations of this position? How do you evaluate performance?

Third, there's no guarantee you won't be let go if you join *any* company.

Conduct a thorough investigation of the company, how it treats people, its reputation and how performance is measured.

IS IT OK TO USE HUMOR IN AN INTERVIEW?

An interview is a time for you and the interviewer to learn. And having fun is an important part of learning. But the fun part needs to be tempered with a presentation of facts and information.

You can answer some questions with humor—just don't be flippant. Then follow up with a more serious response. Example:

You're asked, "What are your weaknesses?" You could reply, "My wife says I'm not a very good cook." Then I'd continue with, "But seriously, I had felt that I lacked formal management training, so when I took over this department I enrolled myself in an extensive management class that meets every Saturday. I definitely feel as if I'm building up that knowledge now."

Remember the example I just gave of someone who's asked a question about compensation—something she didn't know about? She could say:

"My human resource expertise has focused on training and development. I have had some exposure in the area of compensation, but it is limited. However, it is an area I'd be interested in knowing more about. And I really like being compensated."

These responses say: I not only have the skills and am open to improving myself, but I'm a warm, genuine person with a sense of humor.

WHAT IF YOU KEEP HEARING THE COMMENT, "YOU'RE OVERQUALIFIED"?

Louis, who was in his late fifties and had been a senior executive, didn't want the responsibilities of managing anymore. Yet when he interviewed for other positions, he said, "The interviewers act like there's something wrong with me for not wanting to have a high-level job."

If you hear something similar, the interviewer is probably concerned you'll be bored or unchallenged and not stay long, or want too much money. If you're hearing it a lot, bring it up before they do—or in case they're thinking it and not saying anything. Example:

"As you can see from my experience, I have been involved in many levels of business, including senior management. At this point of my career I don't feel I need the challenge of management and am seeking a position where I can use my writing/engineering/training skills."

I once read an article in *The Wall Street Journal* of a study of 109 executives who headed Fortune 500 company subsidiaries with an average $250 million in sales. It concluded: Only 36 percent were "very keen" or "extremely keen" about being the big chief. As executives get older ambition seems to wane," said the article.

Many of my clients who are over fifty tell me the same thing.

IS THERE ANYTHING IN PARTICULAR TO BE PREPARED FOR IF YOU'RE INTERVIEWING FOR A JOB OUT OF TOWN?

If you want to move to St. Louis, employers there will question whether you are serious about relocating. So at the very least be ready to address their concern. Better yet, bring it up before they do. Emphatically state in your letters and conversations that you are committed to pulling up stakes. There is a difference between a decision to consider to move and the decision to make a move.

WHAT IF YOU HAVE A BIG GAP BETWEEN JOBS? WILL INTERVIEWERS THINK SOMETHING IS "WRONG" WITH YOU?

It's true that the longer you're unemployed, the harder the search can be from the interviewer's (and your) perspective. A *New York Times* article several years back quoted a management consultant saying, "A year is almost some sort of grace period. A prospective employer is willing to attribute that to a tough economy. But eighteen months is when it starts to get dicey."

It gets dicey because it can take its toll on your confidence. So get involved in a volunteer activity or do freelance work or consulting. This also tells the interviewer you haven't been sitting at home all day watching soap operas.

HOW DO YOU OVERCOME THE STIGMA OF BEING WITH THE SAME COMPANY YOUR ENTIRE CAREER?

Who said it's a stigma? Look up the word in the dictionary. It means "a mark or token of infamy, disgrace or reproach." Is that how you see your service to this company?

If you do, you've been listening to too many negative thinkers and it's going to sabotage you. It might be true that *some* employers perceive long-time employment with the same company as negative. This perception exists because of how companies and employees have survived for the past decades.

As I talked about in chapter one, many companies

used to reward the status quo. Today, to compete in an increasingly competitive, international market, growing companies encourage experimentation and risk-taking. Some people feel if you've had a "secure" job with one company your entire career, you can't adapt and won't be willing to take necessary risks. They may believe you don't have the right attitude to succeed in today's business world.

But not every employer sees it that way. So first, abandon the idea that being with the same company is a hindrance or mark on your career.

Second, accept the choice you made to stay with this company. Dwell on the positive aspects that are a result of your longevity. These include the wealth of experience you gained, the broad exposure you have to the industry and your scope of knowledge about every aspect of the business.

Third, most likely you've had different jobs in this company, have relocated or been in different functions. Play this up.

Fourth, show employers you're willing to be more entrepreneurial and are continually open to learning.

YOU'RE NO SPRING CHICKEN

What if you're over forty? I lumped this question together with all the other "perceived liability" questions in chapter six. But since it is such a frequent concern, it get its own space here. It's my book, I can do those kinds of things.

This question is based on the rumor going around that if you're older than forty, you're going to have a tough, if not impossible time, getting hired. People in their forties and older started it. When they haven't gotten job offers or interviews, they conclude "It's because of my age." What else could it be?

I'm not saying that some people don't have a legitimate beef. Discrimination against "older" workers does exist. But you don't have to be a victim or let that become an excuse.

Part of the problem is that many forty-plus-year-olds have a tough time in the job market because they fit the stereotype of the "older worker." It's not that they're too old chronologically. But they're not up-to-date technologically, they demonstrate an inflexible attitude, and many times they're resentful they have to start over at this point in their life.

Companies don't want to hire twenty-five-year-olds like that either.

Stay current in how you look, how you think and what you know. Bring up all the reasons you would make a good employee. And don't listen to rumors. (See chapter six.)

Turn your perceived liability into a strength. If you were around during the Reagan/Mondale presidential debates you might remember how smoothly former President Reagan handled such an attack. Mondale brought up the age issue, saying something to the effect that if Reagan was elected, he'd be up in age by his second term. Reagan came back with a comment about not being able to help it if he had more maturity and experience than his opponent. The age issue never came up again during the campaign.

WHAT WOULD YOU NEED TO BE PREPARED FOR IF YOU WERE LAID OFF?

If you were riding high in April and shot down in May, you could hear probing questions to get at how you feel about your situation or how committed you'll be. Examples:

- How do you feel about your company now?
- You must feel pretty angry.
- Will you go back if they call you? This gets asked of people who have worked for that one company most of their careers and the company is the main employer in the area. The concern is that you'll leave the minute you get the chance to go back.

Be cautious about how you respond to the question asking why you left your company or how you feel about the company now. Many people who get laid off feel justified expressing their frustration. Here is an example of how one man responded to the question about why he was no longer with his company:

"This company drove itself into the ground. They put people in key positions that couldn't decide what to have for breakfast, let alone how to spend a thirty million dollar budget. We were loyal. But they just got rid of us."

I give examples of better responses in chapters four and six.

Show interviewers you are a responsible, mature

person who has a realistic outlook. Show them the past is just that. Now you're concentrating on your future.

IS IT OK TO SMOKE OR TELL AN EMPLOYER YOU'RE A SMOKER?

Don't smoke during interviews. Meals are another thing. Don't smoke there either, unless you're both smokers and the interviewer says, "Do you smoke? I'm going to have a cigarette now, why don't we both have one?" But I'd only do it at the end of your meal.

One man wrote to me saying he had been in the running for a job that he really wanted. It was down to him and two other people. The company chose someone else. He wondered if, since he was more qualified than the others, the fact that he smoked influenced the company's decision. How did the interviewer know? The man had a pack of cigarettes in his shirt pocket, which they probably noticed. They don't miss much.

It's possible that was the clincher. Many companies today have no-smoking policies and are not as tolerant of smokers as they used to be. The lesson: Don't leave your cigarettes where they're visible.

IF YOU'RE DISABLED, WHAT SHOULD YOU BE PREPARED FOR? SHOULD YOU TELL EMPLOYERS UP FRONT?

A man with a successful twenty-five-year employment history wrote me this question after he took early retirement due to a downsizing. He had multiple sclerosis and walked with a cane and occasionally used a wheelchair. He also wondered whether he should offer his services without pay until he proved himself.

• Anyone with a disability should be familiar with the Americans with Disabilities Act (ADA), which lists regulations employers must follow. Call the Equal Employment Opportunity Commission Publications and Information Office for "A Technical Assistance Manual on the Employment Provisions of Title I of ADA." It sounds technical, but the office assures me it's in plain English. They're at (800) 669-3362.

• Work without pay? Why would you? Sometimes people doing internships work without pay for a cou-

ple weeks. But I can't think of why *you* should. Your disability shouldn't enter into it.

• As a general guide, if you can perform the essential functions of the job, the employer can't discriminate against hiring you. They can ask you whether you can do a particular task.

Do you tell the interviewer up front? It depends what you mean by up front. A woman who used a wheelchair told me she believed it helped if she let employers know in advance that she was disabled. But she only shared this information because she wanted to *and after* she got the interview. Don't mention it during a prescreening telephone call, on your resumé or in correspondence.

IF YOU'RE PREGNANT AND JOB HUNTING, SHOULD YOU MENTION IT?

The Pregnancy Discrimination Act says an employer cannot refuse to hire a woman because of her pregnancy-related condition as long as she is able to perform the major functions of the job . . . or because of its prejudices against pregnant workers or the prejudices of co-workers, clients or customers.

So in theory there's no problem and no reason not to mention your condition. But let's look at reality and examine your options.

Option 1: You mention it. If you do, be sure to include that you are committed to continue working in the position for which you're being considered after the birth of your child. (That's assuming you're not just looking for a job for the next nine months.)

Option 2: You don't mention it. If you get the job, it will eventually become evident. But at least you got the job. Some people would say this is subscribing to the "What they don't know won't hurt them" philosophy.

Now, the downsides to these options:

Option 1: Being totally honest. Armed with this information, the employer may consciously or subconsciously eliminate you from the running. The employer may have his or her own prejudices about your ability to work while you're pregnant—even though the law says the employer can't act on these. Based on a past experience—or for no reason at all—they may believe you won't come back after you give birth. Employers won't tell you any of that, of course, unless they're very uninformed.

The following is an excerpt from an Ohio court case that was decided in 1994, *El Grande Steak House v. Ohio Civil Rights Commission*, in which the court ruled that pregnancy discrimination had occurred. It is part of the tape-recorded conversation between the employee and the employer and was used as evidence.

Employee: "Okay. Anyway, I found out that I am pregnant . . ."

Employer: ". . . And see, when they see when you're in that condition we don't issue you a bigger skirt. And you need one. And that's not good for the baby to be in that tight leather skirt and carrying trays and being on your feet. And we don't want to kill anybody's child. And that's what you'd be doing. This isn't the type of work that you should be doing when you're having a baby . . ."

Employee: "Well, I—it doesn't matter because it's . . ."

Employer: "It matters to me . . ."

Employee: ". . . I'm still capable of working."

Employer: "Because what if you get sick during the holidays and you can't come in. And you may. You don't know how you're going to act. . . . I can't protect your job to the end, and you may just up and quit any time."

Employee: Well, I would give you notice . . ."

Employer: "You're not going to be able to give me notice if you're sick . . ."

Option 2: You don't bring it up. There may be a lingering question in the employer's mind: Did she know when I hired her? There's the possibility that a feeling of mistrust could develop if he or she believes you knew and didn't say anything. (Not that you were obligated to say anything.) In addition, you may feel bad about not bringing it up.

So what's the answer? This is a very personal decision. You may want to heed my advice to job hunters everywhere about any question: Don't volunteer any information that can be used to discriminate against you. If you do share this information, you may be screened out because of it. On the other hand, you just may not be qualified for the job. But if you think you've been discriminated against, it's an uphill battle to prove it.

On the other hand, you have to do what's right

for you. Weigh the pros and cons and let your conscience be your guide.

For more information on pregnancy discrimination and other issues affecting women in the workforce, call the Women's Bureau Clearinghouse at (800) 827-5335.

WHAT IF YOU SPENT THE FIRST PART OF YOUR CAREER IN ONE AREA, THEN MOVED INTO A FIELD UNRELATED TO THAT OR YOUR EDUCATION AND NOW WANT TO GO BACK TO YOUR ORIGINAL OCCUPATION?

Author Bernard Gunther said: "There is a positive side and negative side; at each moment you decide." In this case you could look at the last five years of your career as not relating to your new career goal and detracting from your value.

Or you could see the positive side: The last five years enhance your attractiveness because you have a broader perspective and more experience.

In interviews, focus on achievements in your first position. Get more education and update yourself in the field you used to be in and tell the interviewer about it.

Out of the Question: What's None of Their Business

I'd have enough money for a down payment on a new car if I had a dollar for every time someone asked me: "But what about when they ask 'How old are you?' or 'Are you married?' Isn't that illegal?"

Let me start by saying that these so-called "illegal questions" may be the thing you're most concerned about, but may be something you never have to deal with. But I know you're wondering about them anyway, and in case you do face them, let's talk about it.

An official from the Equal Employment Opportunity Commission (EEOC) told me: "As far as discussion of religion, for example, in an interview goes, it's not illegal—especially if you're offering the information." But it is unlawful for a company to ask your religion, either on an application or verbally. It is against the law for a person to be denied a job because of religion.

Other books will say some questions are downright unlawful and give a list of things you "can" and "cannot" ask in job interviews. But after talking with civil rights department officials, they tell me that whether questions are unlawful or not can vary from state to state or depend on the context in which they arise.

So I feel more comfortable broadly referring to these questions as unacceptable or inappropriate. If you want to know the exact law where you live, check with the civil rights department in your state or the EEOC.

Let's Get our Priorities Straight

Here's what I think is the most important thing for you to know when it comes to these questions, and *all* questions for that matter: You are being interviewed so that the company can discover whether you are the right person for the job based on skills, experience and education that are necessary for the job. That's it, plain and simple. And that's what they should be asking you about.

It gets sticky when interviewers start poking their noses into subjects *they* think may help them decide if you'll work out.

For example, let's say an interviewer is concerned that if you have kids you'll be late or call in sick a lot or spend too much time on personal calls. And if the job calls for travel he wants to make sure you have someone to take care of the kids when you're out of town. So he asks, "Do you have children?"

Now, does whether you have children or not have *anything* to do with the skills, experience or education necessary to do the job? No. So why is he asking? He thinks, as I just said, it could affect your ability to do the job—that you won't be as committed, will be distracted or unable to do the job.

This is an example of an unacceptable or inappropriate question because it has nothing to do with what you should be evaluated on: your skills, experience and education to do the job. So, you need to address his fears about your commitment level and ability to do your job—kids or no kids.

"Wait a minute," you're saying, "why should I address *his* fears? He's not supposed to ask that question in the first place!"

You're right. He's out of line. By law he shouldn't have those concerns, let alone ask about them. So you have two choices here.

You could make it an issue. Let me help you.

Here are some of the ways you can do that. You could say:

1. You can't ask that!
2. I resent that question.
3. How dare you ask about my personal life!
4. That's none of your damn business.

What could happen? Well, the interview might go down the toilet. Most probably—even though you're justified in your reaction—you can say farewell to any interest he has in you.

And if you believe you weren't hired in response to such an improper question, you may find yourself contacting an attorney or the Civil Rights Commission in your state.

or

You could choose to maintain the good rapport you've developed and keep the interview process intact, yet assert yourself in an appropriate way. If that's what you want to do, here's how to handle this sensitive situation.

1. Decide if you want to answer the question. Some people don't mind answering these types of questions.

For example, Angela told me she was very forthright about the fact that she had a young child. "Even though I knew they weren't supposed to ask, I wanted them to know what kind of person I am, so during lunch I talked about family when they asked."

2. On the other hand, if you hear a question that doesn't seem appropriate and don't want to answer it, ask yourself: Does this question have anything to do with my ability to perform the job?

In most cases it won't, so your response should be something to that effect. The trick is handling it with firm diplomacy.

For example, if you're asked, "Do you plan to have children?" you can respond with: "If my spouse and I do choose to have a family, we certainly won't be seeking to disrupt the company."

My favorite technique is to turn the question back to the interviewer, asking, "Why do you ask?" or "I'm not sure what that would have to do with my being qualified for the position. Could you explain?"

When you handle these delicate situations like this, you will not get an Academy Award for your brilliant dramatic performance, but you will get an *A* for diplomacy, tact and for acting like a professional. And you can always seek legal assistance if you believe you were denied a position because of your response to one of these inappropriate questions.

Now if the question is so outrageous it may not require such diplomacy. In fact, you probably wouldn't want to work for the company. An example—I swear this is the honest truth—is the time two women, in two different situations, and by different employers, were asked what kind of birth control they used. Both of them high-tailed it out of the interview the minute they heard that question.

It's Beginning to Sound a Lot Like Discrimination

As a general guide, don't offer information that is irrelevant. If you do, it is very difficult to prove that you have been discriminated against because, as I said earlier, you offered it.

Stick to information that demonstrates you have the skills, experience and education to do the job.

If you're asked something that sounds off alarms in you, assert yourself appropriately.

The chart on page 110 lists questions employers may and may not ask.

CHECKLIST

✔ Know your skills and work experience, how and why you've been successful and have stories to prove it.
✔ Share the facts, then stop talking.
✔ Know "what you know" (your knowledge and expertise), how you learned it, how you stay current and how you'll make a difference, and have stories to prove it.
✔ Know what kind of person you are and how you handle things, situations and people, and have stories to prove it.
✔ Stick to information that demonstrates you have the skills, experience and education to do the job.
✔ Know what questions are appropriate and inappropriate for employers to ask.
✔ If you hear inappropriate questions but you want to keep the interview on track, ask what the question has to do with the job.
✔ Always take the high road when answering questions.
✔ As good as you think you are, plan your answers and practice, practice, practice.

QUESTION EMPLOYERS "MAY ASK"	QUESTIONS EMPLOYER "MAY NOT ASK"	MAY ASK	MAY NOT ASK
What is your full name? Have you ever worked for the Gerry Company under a different name?	What's your original name? Have you ever changed your name or used another name? What's your maiden name?	Do you have any physical or mental impairments that would interfere with your ability to perform this job?	Do you have a disability?
Are you at least eighteen?	How old are you? What is your birth date?	What type of education do you have?	
Are you a U.S. citizen? How long have you lived in this city or state?	Where were you born? Where were your parents or spouse born?	What schools have you attended?	
What languages do you speak or write fluently?	What's your native tongue? How did you acquire the ability to speak, read or write a foreign language?	What is your work experience?	
		Are you related to anyone who works here?	
	Are you married? What is your spouse's name? Does your spouse work? Do you have children? Who takes care of them? What are their ages?	Have you ever been convicted of a crime other than misdemeanors?	
	What is your race?	What organizations do you belong to (not including those that indicate race, religion or ancestry)?	
	What is your religion? What are your religious customs and holidays?	What service have you been in in the U.S. Armed Forces?	Did you ever serve in the military for any country other than the United States? What type of discharge did you get?
	How tall are you? How much do you weigh?		
	Do you go by Mr., Miss, Ms. or Mrs.? (or any question about gender, ability to reproduce or advocacy of any type of birth control)		

CHAPTER 10

Driving a Hard Bargain

Strategy #10

**When negotiating, keep quiet
and ask for what you want at the right
time and you'll probably get it.**

Money is such a sticky subject. On the one hand, it's nobody's business. But there you are anyway, sitting down with perfect strangers telling them what you made before, what you make now and what you want to make if you work for them.

In some cases you're not even eyeball to eyeball. They call you up and say, "Hello, I'm Harvey Haveley and I'm calling in response to your letter for the job here at the Bert & Eve Company." After a few moments of chitchat, he says, "Could you tell me what your salary is now?" or "What are your salary expectations?" And away you go blabbing information you wouldn't dream of telling anyone else.

Why do you do it? Because they ask. Because you don't want to offend them. Because you think they'll hang up if you don't tell them and you'll never get a shot at the job. You figure they need to know, or they wouldn't be asking, right?

Just for the record, they don't need to know. They just *want* to know. But more on that later.

Go back and look at the second sentence of this chapter. That's right—your salary is nobody's business. The only thing the interviewer needs to know is what your skills, talents, experience and expertise are and why you're qualified for the job. Later, much, much later, it *may* be time to talk about money.

So in this chapter, you'll learn how to explore a job opening without divulging salary information, like good wine, before its time—or ever. You'll learn

how to get offers not because you're the right price, but because you're the right person for the job.

You'll also learn how to to ask for what you do want—and, hopefully, get it.

MUCH ADO ABOUT MONEY

I just want to say up front that this money issue gets way too much attention. It is not your priority—or at least it shouldn't be. No, really. Think about it. Would you take any job just for the money—even if it meant you'd be miserable?

I've had clients making triple-digit figures who were so down in the dumps and dispirited they were ready to throw it all out the window (some did) just for peace of mind, time with their family or to save their marriage. Money can't buy you love.

So first, let's put money in its right place. You have to like what you do, be challenged, be in a comfortable environment, work for a company you believe in and whose values you support, and finally, be fairly compensated for your contribution. Remember the nine key elements? *All* of those make up The Job You Want. (That's what the first eight chapters were about.)

If you remember that, then every time the interviewer brings up money, you can say something to that effect. We'll get into more specific wording later.

Money can be a big issue for the employer, but don't let it be for you. Why is it an issue for them? Well, they may be using it as screening criteria. They're thinking: "We need to find out if she fits into what we have in mind. Is she too expensive? Or is she too cheap (underqualified)? If she's either, we don't want to waste time on her."

So if you are either—too expensive *or* too cheap—you could get weeded out before they even know how wonderful you are. If they only knew this first (how terrific you are) they may have been willing to pay more to get you.

So first you have to establish your value. More on this later, as well.

Even So, Let's Talk

Having said all that, we still need to discuss this issue of money because:

1. It will come up, as I said, as early as the first phone call, possibly in the first interview and definitely if they're interested in you.

2. You need to be able to deal with it so it doesn't sabotage the process.

3. To get what you want you need to know how to negotiate.

Since it usually becomes an issue with the interviewer—possibly even a sore spot—you need to be well equipped to handle it.

Let's Negotiate

It's not a dirty word. In fact, you've been learning how to negotiate since chapter three. The negotiations begin when:

- You send your first letter to the employer
- They hear your voice on the phone
- You walk into their offices, shake hands and smile

These are their very first impressions of you and that's when you begin to build your value.

The negotiations continue as:

- You handle the questions we just covered in chapter nine
- You write the employer a letter and proposal and you follow up

These are all ways you demonstrate your confidence, professionalism, ability to communicate, attitude, enthusiasm and all the other things they scrutinize. You have to establish your value before you have any negotiating strength—that is, to ask

for and get what you want. That's the first part of negotiating.

WHAT YOU'RE NEGOTIATING FOR

The best package you can get (this includes more than money) in exchange for everything you bring to the table. For now, let's just talk about money.

Money Matters

You want to be paid the best price for what you have to offer—what is fair and competitive.

You know what is fair and competitive because you researched the market. This is tough to put an exact figure on, because labor is intangible. So you fit into a range. You'll get paid according to how complicated the job is and the level of responsibilities.

They, on the other hand, are smart and thinking: "I know I have to pay quality prices for quality people. But, I'm going to try to get the best quality for the lowest price." Can you blame them?

No sweat. Just go in equipped.

Walk in the door with:

1. A PROMISE TO YOURSELF

I will not discuss salary until I've been offered the position.

I will not discuss salary until I've been offered the position.

I will not discuss salary until I've been offered the position.

Say this five hundred times.

Why don't you want to discuss salary until then? To explain, I'll use an analogy that most everyone can identify with.

Let's say you found a lost puppy. You really didn't want a new dog. You're never home, dogs have to be taken to the vet, you have to walk them. They can get costly. But being the kindhearted soul that you are, you take it in the house and start calling your friends to find it a home. Three days later, you still haven't found it a home. By now, he's got a name. Fluffy fetches your slippers and the morning paper. He greets you when you come home with his big brown eyes and wagging tail. He makes you feel good. You even met a new friend in the park when you were walking him. On the fourth day, you decide Fluffy is worth it. You're going to keep him, no matter what he costs you. He has proved his worth.

You are like this puppy to the employer. One of the main issues on her mind is, "He's going to cost me. I better find out if I can afford him before we get attached—before I spend more time and money."

So, like Fluffy, you must endear yourself to the employer. Show her why you're worth what you command. Get her to see how much better life would be with you in it. You start doing this—that is, establishing your value—the second you meet her. That's why the negotiating has already begun.

Your goal is to take the focus off what you're going to cost her and show her your worth—whatever that is. So promise yourself you won't talk about money until she's sold. How will you know she's sold? When she offers you the job.

2. WHAT YOU'D LOVE TO MAKE AND WHAT YOU'LL SETTLE FOR

You need to go into the interview with two figures in mind:

1. The salary that would make you thoroughly ecstatic.
2. The lowest salary you'll settle for (This would be a figure that's nothing to sneeze at: it's more than what you were making, it's fair, but it's not fantastic.)

How do you get these figures? Look at your research. What's the range for this type of position and where do you fit in?

Let's say you're a software engineer. You found out they get paid about $33,000 starting out, and can get up to $75,520. Based on your experience, you're somewhere in the middle.

So you decide that you'd go dancing in the streets if they offered you $60,000. But if you like the job and everything else enough, you'd go as low as $52,000. You're not doing anything with this information yet. We'll get back to it. For now, just keep it tucked in the negotiating crevices of your brain.

3. KEY PHRASES TO DEAL WITH THEIR PROBING

Yes, most interviewers will do what they can to find out what kind of money you are looking for in your next position, what you're making now or were

making in your last job. Expect these questions. Be ready to hear them:

On the phone. I went into detail in chapter three on how to handle this when I discussed screening techniques. Bottom line: Don't give any figures. If you feel pressed, give a range. Tell them you'd like to meet and learn more about the position.

At your first or second interview. The interviewer might say: "What kind of salary are you looking for?"

Here are some phrases to put in your own words:

"Although money is an important issue, it's not my priority. What's most important to me is to explore whether I'd be using my strengths and making a difference here at your firm. I really don't know enough about the position to be able to answer that at this point. It seems as though it would make sense to discuss salary once we decide I'm right for the position."

The interviewer might also ask: "What were you making at your last job?" or "What are you making now?" This is irrelevant and has nothing to do with this new position. You'll say something like that, only more tactfully:

"My position at the Florence Company is different than this one at your company. It's really a different set of circumstances. I hesitate to share my present compensation because we're probably not comparing apples with apples. In addition, I think it's important to look at total compensation, which would depend on the scope of the position. It would help if we could talk more about the position."

What if the employer says, "This position pays such-and-such, is that acceptable?" If the salary is outrageously low, you probably just found out you're interviewing for the wrong position. But if it's in the ball park, respond with something like:

"At this point, it sounds like we're in the ball park. Could you tell me more about the position?"

When Push Comes to Shove

Is the question "But what if they *persist* in knowing my salary requirements?" lurking in your head?

It is rare that an employer will threaten: "If you don't tell me what you're making, I'm ending this interview." (Although, I have heard of one instance when that did happen. But do you want to work for that kind of a person anyway?)

More likely, the interviewer will coyly continue to bring it up:

"Just so we're in the same ball park, what kind of salary do you want?" Your response:

"I can appreciate the need to discuss salary. I'm sure your company compensates fairly and I'd be happy to look at those ranges. Could you tell me what the range is for this position?"

If he says, "Between $30,000 and $45,000" (or whatever the range is), listen, pause and then—assuming it's accurate—tell him that the higher end of the range is in your ball park. Then get back to talking about the job.

What if he gets a little testy: "We really need to know your salary to continue our discussion." If you sense negative vibes or frustration from the interviewer and feel the relationship is at risk if you don't share something, give a range that would include a total compensation package, and add that you are flexible in discussing the way you come up with that. Ask how that fits into what they are considering.

Oh yes, there's another reason not to mention a figure: You'll be locked into whatever you say and lose the chance to negotiate later.

You Want Me to Do What?

If you're like most people, it may not even occur to you to negotiate. You figure, they're offering me what they can and it's "take it or leave it." You may even think "If I negotiate, one of three things could happen:

1. They'll think I'm pushy.
2. They'll go along with it but resent me once I'm on the job.
3. They'll get mad and withdraw the offer."

Now think about this. If you present your request in an appropriate manner and at the right time, you won't come across as pushy. You are establishing yourself as a professional.

They're not dumb, so they're not going to agree to anything they don't want to or pay through the nose. Again, if you do this *right* (that's a key word), they won't resent you. They'll see you as a professional who knows what she wants.

It's highly, highly unlikely they'll withdraw the offer just because you've countered it. Why would

they? They want you . . . they want to make you happy. They're thinking, what will it take to get you to accept the position?

This idea of negotiating is something we Americans just aren't at home with. When we go to buy something, we look at the price, take whatever it is to the register and fork over the dough.

Other cultures expect there to be some haggling. In fact, a merchant in a street market of another country might be insulted if, after he says, "It will cost you five hundred doodads," you say "OK."

Some people consider negotiating an unnecessary game. "Why don't they just state the offer in the first place?"

Well, they do. But it's the *first* offer—one that usually allows them to pay the lowest reasonable price. Isn't that what every smart businessperson would do?

Your goal is to be paid the most based on your value and get everything else that will make your job there as pleasant as possible. You have to tell them what will make you happy.

Other reasons people don't negotiate is because they don't know how. (We get into that in a few pages.) Or they think, what's the use—it's not negotiable.

JUST WHAT IS NEGOTIABLE?

Negotiating gurus tell you *everything* is negotiable. That could be the case here, too. It all depends on the company, the people you're dealing with and the position.

People who do consider negotiating usually only think to do it with salary and benefits. But there are all kinds of goodies that could be up for grabs.

First let's talk about:

Salary

In today's job market, you need to get creative. Look beyond salary and regular pay raises. These kinds of guarantees are few and far between these days. The trend is toward pay-for-performance. So here's a look at optional pay programs:

• *Incentive pay.* Many companies offer programs in which you can make an extra 10 percent to 30 percent of your salary if you perform big. You can make a pretty penny this way, and it also maximizes your value in your field. Find out what projects are key to the company to explore a pay-for-performance arrangement.

• *Bonuses tied to company performance.* Consider a plan in which your bonus is tied to profit, or to the performance of your division or of the entire company.

• *Look for ways to increase your value.* Do you have unusual skills? Can you do the job of two people? A man called me who had expertise in architectural drawing and project management, saying: "I can do the jobs of two people—does this make me more valuable?" You bet.

Everything But the Kitchen Sink

Now, get out a piece of paper. Write down everything you want in your job. Things that don't cost the employer actual dollars can be more enticing. Here are some ideas:

Free parking	Buying your home if
Child care	you're moving
More vacation days	Job sharing
Flex time	(having shared
Stock options	responsibilities of one
Equity in the company	specific position,
Telecommuting	which usually
(working from	includes part-time
home)	schedules)
A nice, big office at the	Keeping frequent flyer
end of the hall with	miles
a window	Subscriptions to
A computer	publications
Tuition	Seminars
reimbursement	Use of aircraft and car,
Health club	and allowance for
memberships	home and auto
Professional	insurance (these are
memberships	typically given to the
Company car	top money-makers in
Relocation expenses;	the organization)
assistance in job	Severance pay
search for your	Signing bonus
spouse or	Additional reviews
significant other	

Hey, why not ask? The worst that can happen is that they say no. Prioritize these and figure out the ones you're really prepared to ask for.

Carrots Not to Dangle

We are so sales-oriented in this culture, you may think of offering your skills at 20 percent off to get the job. Examples:

• A fifty-six-year-old man who was laid off from his job said an employer asked him if he had a pension. "I was caught off guard and gave an answer. I suppose the one good thing is that if I do have a pension the employer may see me as more desirable."

This man assumes the employer sees him as more desirable because, due to his pension, he'll want a lower salary. You don't need to lower your standards to make yourself more attractive. Also, whether you have a pension or not is irrelevant and has nothing to do with whether you are the right person for the job. If you are asked this, say, "Why do you ask?"

• A woman wrote me saying the interviewer asked her: "What do you feel you can bring to the company and what are the advantages of hiring you?" She replied: "The fact that I don't need benefits since I am covered by my husband's company."

I suppose this could be an added plus, but certainly not the reason to hire her. The interviewer is asking about the skills she has and how she's going to make the business better . . . how she'll contribute to the bottom line.

Other times people offer unsolicited and irrelevant information:

• One man told me, "I wanted the interviewer to know I was being honest when I told him my salary range, so I offered to show them my W-2 forms." You shouldn't be talking about past income, let alone producing proof of it.

Not Negotiable? Think Again

Some companies have policies with pay ranges that are hard to budge. Government jobs are like that—they have specific categories that you fit into. Yes, this makes your negotiating job tougher, but not impossible.

See if you can qualify for another category based on other experience you've had. Does your volunteer work increase your value? For example, remember the man who was the building contractor and wanted to be an advertising account executive? He was able to show that his volunteer work running political campaigns gave him years of marketing experience. He got a higher salary than he would have just starting out as a junior account executive.

You could also suggest a different job title (that does offer more money) or create a new title for an expanded role that's worth more.

LET'S REVIEW:

✔ You've got your two figures in mind:
The one that would make you jump for joy and the one you'll settle for.
  ✔ You've got your key phrases etched in your mind.

If she says, "So what kind of salary are you looking for?" what do you say? (It's OK to cheat—for now. Turn back to point three under key phrases.)

But for the interview you *must* know this language so you don't stumble and sound confused. Which you will. If you don't practice, you'll sound like my clients when we role-play for the first time:

I say: "So what kind of salary are you looking for?"

They say: "Well, I like money, I certainly want to talk about it at some point, but you know, it wouldn't seem right to talk about it yet . . . I mean I think it would all depend . . . and I don't know at this time if we know enough about things . . . and we need to compare apples and apples, and I'd just rather tell you other things first . . . why don't we wait until later?"

Sometimes they go to the other extreme:

"I don't think we should be talking about that yet."

Practice, practice, practice.

  ✔ You've got your promise to yourself:
I will not discuss salary until I've been offered the position.
  ✔ You agree that you're not going to get what you don't ask for. Right?
  ✔ You understand that they're not going to throw you out of the office for having a mature, adult, give-and-take conversation about what they're offering and what you want. Right?

  ✔ You've thought through some alternative salary plans and ways to enhance your value.
  ✔ You've written down all the things you want, besides money.

Good. You're equipped.

SOUNDS OF SILENCE (AND OTHER THINGS TO SAY AND DO)

Pretend you're in your third interview with the Mitchell S. Company. In your second meeting, the person who would be your manager asked about salary. But with grace and elegance, you were able to deter that discussion. Now they're interested in you and you're definitely interested in them. Your research turned up a salary range for the position of $30,000 to $42,000. You feel you fit in somewhere between $34,000 and $37,000.

There are a jillion different scenarios that could happen from this point on. I'll cover the most common ones and the questions people usually ask about.

Scenario One

Employer:

"Fabian, we'd like to have you on board here. The position pays $30,000. The benefits package is what is outlined in the employee handbook."

Yes, it's now OK to discuss the money issue. Why? Because she offered you the job. You may want to jump up from your chair and sing a chorus of "Happy Days Are Here Again." Instead, stay seated and say:

"Well, I'm very pleased, Ms. Ina, that you are interested in me. I feel very good about the Mitchell S. Company. I think there's an excellent fit here. Could you tell me a little more about your benefits package?"

She gets into the details. You listen, repeat her salary offer and then sit quietly. During that time, she's wondering what you're thinking. Here's what can happen during the silence:

1. She ups the offer: "We could go to $32,500." If she does, you can either continue to say nothing (silence is a very powerful tool) or go on to scenario two.

2. She explains that the offer is firm: "That's really as high as I can go . . . this position fits within a

pay range and this is what others at this level are making." Move to scenario two.

3. She plays good guy, bad guy: "That's all I've been authorized to offer. I could check with Muriel, my boss, though, to see if there's any flexibility." You say: "I'm really excited about working here. I'd appreciate that."

4. She notices you haven't said anything more, so she says something like:

"How does that sound, Fabian?" Move to scenario two.

Scenario Two

You: "I'm really pleased you feel there's a good fit here. I know I'd enjoy working here. I'm sure you want to compensate me with a salary that will keep me productive. (She might nod.) Well, based on my research, my background, qualifications and value I bring to the position, I feel your offer is on the low side."

Your options, depending on how she reacts next:

1. She says: "Did you have a figure in mind?"

You: "Based on my research, I'm thinking somewhere in the range of $35,000 to $40,000." You'll notice this is higher than where you feel you fit in. Here's why: If she offers you $38,000—which you'd be pleased as punch about—you are demonstrating your willingness to compromise, since $40,000 was the high end; if she offers you $35,000, she's still come up, it's still more than your lowest figure and you'd be satisfied.

It will be tempting to just name a figure. Don't. Give a range.

2. She could still come back and say that's all she can offer in the form of base salary. But perhaps there's a way to get you into their stock options plan, incentive pay program or profit sharing. Ask to hear more about that or if that's a possibility. Tell her you're open to being creative about compensation.

This is also a good time to bring up some of the key projects for the company and tie in a pay-for-performance arrangement.

Scenario Three

What if the first figure she mentions is exactly what you had in mind? Although it's not likely, since she'll probably start low, think about it for a minute and say: "Your offer is very fair. Could we plan on a six-month evaluation that includes a salary review?" Also suggest that the two of you sit down and develop the specific goals and objectives you'd be expected to meet. Get all of this in writing.

If you haven't discussed benefits yet, do it now. Bring up the things on your list. When you do, show the employer how it will help her. For example:

"I understand your policy is to give one week's vacation the first year. My experience has always been that I work long hours and am very dedicated and I need to rejuvenate my creativity more often. Several breaks over a year's time works best, so I would like to look at two weeks of vacation my first year."

HOW AND WHEN TO ACCEPT

Let's figure that you've come to an agreement on the salary and the entire package. What next? *Take your time.* Take at least twenty-four hours to think about the offer and get back to them. Take longer if you need it. Never make a decision at the time the offer is made. It appears—and is—unprofessional to decide on the spot.

Summarize, once again, your excitement about the job, tell them you'd like to think about it and get back to them. Ask when they need your answer.

If they press you for an answer on the spot or aren't willing to give you a reasonable amount of time to consider the offer, I'd reconsider working for the company. A reasonable amount of time is anywhere from a day to a week. Some of my clients have asked for up to two and three weeks.

In the meantime, here's what you're doing while you're thinking about the offer:

- Talking it over with your spouse, significant other, friend or relative. He or she might offer a viewpoint you hadn't considered.
- Gaining objectivity. It's flattering to be wanted. Also, if you've been looking for awhile and you finally have an offer you like, it's tempting to grab it without thinking everything through.
- Conducting a final analysis of the job and how it compares to your nine key elements.
- Thinking through any other questions you have about the position.
- Speeding up other potential offers (I'll talk about that in a minute).

What to Evaluate

THE POSITION

- Are the responsibilities challenging?
- Will you be using your strengths?
- Will you be doing what motivates you and what you like to do?
- What's the growth potential?
- Will you get satisfaction from this job?

THE SALARY

- Is it what you want?
- What's the potential?
- Is there a bonus or incentive?

THE BENEFITS

- How's the overall package?

THE COMPANY

- Do you believe in its product or service?
- Does it have a good reputation among its employees, competitors and others outside the company?
- Are the company's values in line with yours?
- Is the company mission something you can believe in?

THE ENVIRONMENT

- Is it where you'll be most productive?
- Does it feel comfortable?

THE PEOPLE

- Do you feel comfortable with the person you'd be working for?
- How do you feel about the people you'd work with or your staff?

Not all of these factors will be equally important. And no position will be perfect. Look at each of these areas and write down the pros and cons so you can see how the position rates.

Be objective. Sit with this information. Decisions like this need to be discovered by thorough evaluation. You owe it to yourself and the company to be sure this is the job for you.

THE PLOT THICKENS: BEFORE YOU SIGN ON THE DOTTED LINE

If there's anything you thought of that needs to be addressed, now's the time to bring it up. Here are some issues that my clients have experienced:

Celebrate, Celebrate

What if you celebrate holidays that are different than the ones the company pays you to take off? One man, who celebrates different religious holidays than most people, wanted to take days off that would be regular working days for everyone else. He was hesitant to mention it before he was hired. At the same time he was afraid that if he didn't bring it up now, the company wouldn't give him those days off.

Situations like this are very personal, so how you handle it will be based on your own beliefs. Most companies have policies that allow for time off for American or Christian holidays. Companies are required by law to "reasonably accommodate" what are called "sincerely held" religious beliefs. Most of them will also respect other holidays and be flexible about time off if they understand the situation either before or after someone is hired.

Others will have stricter policies that require you to take vacation time or time without pay. Many companies offer paid personal days, which can be used. Some companies even have "holiday swapping." This might allow someone who has a strong feeling for Martin Luther King Day (a holiday the company doesn't give as a paid holiday) to swap Presidents Day, for example.

If you get an offer, then bring up this issue and the company withdraws the offer, the employer would appear to be discriminating against you.

Three Weddings, a Funeral and a Vacation

What if you planned your vacation long before you interviewed for this job and you want to accept the position? Tell the employer about your plans. Say:

"I'd like to accept the position. But there is one concern. My family and I have already planned our two-week vacation at the end of the summer. I know your policy is to take vacations after you've been here six months. And I will only have been on the job three months by then."

Just don't spring the news your first day on the job and expect them to honor your request. Mention it when you're discussing how and when you'll begin employment. You're in a negotiating position now—when the employer is most inclined to accommodate you.

A Baby in the Offing

One of my clients knew she and her husband would be starting a family over the next five years. So it was important for her to find out about maternity issues. Research your company's maternity leave policy. If you work for a company that has fifty employees or more, the passage of the Family and Medical Leave Act of 1993 could affect your situation. In essence it provides for up to twelve weeks of unpaid leave to workers who need to care for a new child or deal with a serious medical condition affecting them or other family members.

FROM FAMINE TO FEAST: WHEN THERE'S TWO (POTENTIAL OR FIRM) OFFERS

What if they're really anxious to get someone in the position and want your answer, but you're not ready because you've got another offer pending or there's a good chance of another offer from a second company?

Should you tell the first company you need more time? Do you mention the other offer to the second company?

It's best to:

1. Tell the company that made the firm offer that you've been on an active search and will need time to consider it. Stress that you want this to be the right decision for everyone . . . that you wouldn't want to make a hasty decision and come on board until you felt it was absolutely right . . . that although you feel there's a good fit, you would like to consider the offer for a longer period.

2. In the meantime, see what you can do about speeding up the potential offers. Go back to the second company and explain the situation: That you've been offered another position and are sharing this information with them in the event that they would

want to accelerate their decision-making. They may or may not be able to do anything.

Let the Bidding Begin

If you do get down to two offers that are running neck and neck in terms of what you want, stand back from both and check the small, but possibly significant, things. Ask yourself: What particulars did I pick up on that gave me insight into the company? How did those affect me?

For example, Mark received two offers that were very similar, but noticed that one company never tried to sell him on coming there. "They didn't put an incentive package in the offer. When I asked about it, they said, 'We just take that for granted.' They also spelled my name wrong in the letter. The other company paid for a visit for my entire family before the offer came. That company seemed to be more concerned about me. These things made a difference."

Listen to your intuition.

How to Say No

As diplomatically as possible. In Lee's case, it was so close, it came down to the locations of the company—and that's what he told them. Say something like:

"I am very flattered by your offer. I'm impressed with your company and know I'd enjoy this job. I've given this a lot of thought over the last few days. It has come down to a matter of which city my family and I want to be in. We really do want to be in Seattle, so I have decided to take the other offer. I want to thank you again for your interest in me."

HOW SWEET IT IS TO BE HIRED BY YOU: GET IT IN WRITING

This confirms the offer and company's commitment to you. This is especially important if you're leaving your old job. You want to make sure there's a job waiting for you.

Ask them to type the offer and everything they agreed to in a letter (see sample on pages 120-121). Most large companies do this through their human resources department. If you're dealing with a smaller company, this may not be something they normally do, so you can offer to write and submit it yourself.

Arcade Shoes and More Shoes
14 Main Street
Logan, Ohio 43138

Ms. Leila Howard
1070 Annavicki Way
Philadelphia, Pennsylvania 19101

Dear Leila,

We are pleased to confirm our offer of employment to you to join Arcade Shoes and More Shoes. As discussed, your title will be Assistant Buyer.

COMPENSATION:

Your initial salary will be $2,500 per month to be paid on a twice-monthly basis.

In addition, you will receive a one-time signing bonus of $5,000 less taxes, which is contingent upon your continued employment status for one year. You will receive the check within two weeks following your hire date. If you leave Arcade during your first year of employment, or are terminated for cause, you will be required to reimburse Arcade for this amount on a pro rata basis.

BENEFITS:

Arcade offers a variety of benefit programs to assist you in caring for you and your family. These benefits include time away from work, health care plans and capital accumulation programs. They include:

• Time away from work benefits include twelve holidays per year, vacation, personal business allowance, short- and long-term disability or pay continuation, medical leave, personal leave of absence, military leave of absence and family leave of absence.

• Health care benefit plans include your choice of two medical plans: a Preferred Provider Organization Indemnity Plan or a Health Maintenance Organization; a dental option: the Federated Dental Corporation; a vision plan; long-term disability package and a life insurance program. Other benefits include an Employee Assistance Program, Employee Fitness Center, Wellness Programs, a referral program which helps you identify family education needs, maternity planning, adoption assistance, child care and elder care.

• Capital accumulation programs designed to assist you in preparing for your retirement and other future financial needs include a 401(k) Plan and an Employee Stock Purchase Plan. Please review your benefits handbook for more details about your options as one of our employees. We'll be happy to answer any of your questions. Please call us at 1-800-000-0000.

RELOCATION:

To assist you with your relocation from Philadelphia to Logan, we are offering you relocation benefits as outlined in the attached Corporate Relocation Policy. You will receive up to three nights and four days for House Hunting and thirty days temporary living allowance. Please coordinate your move through Sondra Leeman at 1-800-000-0000.

Sample job offer letter

This offer is contingent upon your successful completion of a medical evaluation, which includes testing for the presence of drugs, proof that you meet the educational requirements of the job, a security background check as stated on the employment application and your ability to provide proof of your eligibility to work in the United States.

This offer is also contingent upon your agreement that if you voluntarily terminate your employment with Arcade within one year following the effective date of your employment, you will reimburse Arcade 100 percent for relocation expenses.

This offer will remain open until March 15, 1996. Enclosed is a detailed list of the information necessary to begin employment with Arcade. Please sign this original letter and return it to me with your start date indicated, as formal acceptance of the offer. We are very pleased to offer you this position and are confident you will make a substantial contribution to Arcade. Please call me at 1-800-000-0000 if you have any questions.

Sincerely,

George Lieberman
Director of Human Resources

Accepted

_____   _____
Signature   Date

_____
Start Date

Sample job offer letter continued

Once you have made your final decision, you can call them on the phone to accept.

Sometimes offers come in person, over the phone, in the mail or a combination of any of those.

Special Circumstances

CONTRACTUAL AGREEMENTS

If a company wants to talk about a contractual or consulting relationship, check with people in your field who may have created a similar working situation. If you don't know anyone who has done that, check with managers in similar businesses and ask them how they have established this kind of arrangement.

Many contractual employees work by the hour. Others work by the project. Ask questions related to this: If you were to hire someone on a contractual basis to handle this type of work, how would you put a dollar amount on their services—by project or by the hour?

Ask what they have in mind in terms of an arrangement. First—just like a full-time position—make sure it's a good working relationship. Then discuss compensation.

Things to consider:

- Benefits probably won't be covered by the employer.
- Who pays for job-related expenses you'll incur if you work at home?
- How will taxes be paid?
- You may work for a limited time or for specific projects with no guarantee of work. When the

work is completed, the contractual arrangement ends.

INEXPERIENCE STILL PAYS

If you're a recent graduate, have little experience in a field, are re-entering the job market after being out awhile or are changing careers, you may think you don't have any experience and, therefore, not much room to negotiate.

That thinking puts you back into the "I'll take what I can get" mentality. If the company didn't see worth in you, it wouldn't offer you a position. You can always acquire knowledge. They're hiring you because of everything else you have—you're smart as a whip, your great attitude, dependability, dedication, intelligence, good humor, all your strengths that have made you successful thus far in life—and they obviously see it. You need to see it as well. That's your negotiating tool and that's what you bring up.

CHECKLIST

✔ Establish your value so the employer wants you and is willing to pay for you.

✔ Don't talk about salary until you're offered the job.

✔ Have two figures in mind: what you'd love to make and what you'll settle for.

✔ Know how to diplomatically handle interviewers' premature questions about salary.

✔ Memorize and practice key phrases to postpone salary discussion and to react to offers. Practice and record yourself.

✔ Make a list of what you want.

✔ Look at optional pay plans.

✔ Don't sell yourself short.

✔ Don't be afraid to ask for what you want.

✔ Know when to keep quiet.

✔ Don't accept or reject an offer on the spot.

✔ Get everything in writing.

✔ Use your head to negotiate, and believe in your heart you can get it.

Once You Get The Job You Want

Sing a few bars of "Happy Days Are Here Again." Go out and celebrate. Take off a few days or even weeks before you start your new job.

But keep that strategic job-hunting thinking cap strapped snugly to your head. Here's how:

1. Write everyone you talked to during your job search a letter to share the good news. Thank them for their help, information, advice and interest—whatever role they played. These people are a part of your network.

If you met with them or talked to them on the phone, they will have an interest in your well-being. In a way, you're closing a chapter by letting them know where you landed, but you're also keeping the book open for future contact and interest. And do keep in contact with them—even if you're not looking for a job.

2. Keep track of your accomplishments in this new job as they occur. This will make it easier for you to update your resumé and build evidence of your value when you want to ask for a raise, or if, in the future, you decide to look for a new job. Just jot them down as they happen.

3. Always hunt for ways to enhance your value in your new organization. It's easy to become complacent. Remember what I talked about way back in chapter three—that you will need to justify your existence and personally impact the company's success . . . solve its changing problems . . . help it be more productive, profitable and thrive in this competitive, customer-oriented, quality-focused marketplace.

No matter what your level in the company, find out what its goals are and ways you can help reach them.

4. Keep communications with your manager open. Initiate regular contact through formal performance evaluations and informal chats about what you're working on and how you're doing. Don't leave this up to the person you work for.

5. Stay updated in your industry. Scout for ways to stay informed and current on new developments, technology and ideas. Seek educational opportunities. This will also keep you refreshed and enthusiastic.

6. Take stock regularly of how you feel about your job. Ask yourself the kinds of questions you did when you were evaluating whether this was the right job for you in the first place. Am I still using my strengths? Am I motivated? Am I still doing what I like to do? Am I growing, challenged, learning? Am I satisfied? Do I still feel good about the company? Am I being productive? Am I valued and recognized for my contributions? If any of these areas need work, do something about it. Don't let it fester. Discover ways to enhance your job.

7. Always be planning your next step—not necessarily your next job. What are you moving toward that will build on your knowledge and experience? What will keep you excited about your work? This is the only way to secure your future and to create The Next Job You Want.

THE NINE KEY ELEMENTS OF THE JOB YOU WANT

A job that:

- Uses your unique talents and skills
- Fits your personality, style and personal characteristics
- Challenges you to think and grow
- Pays you what you're worth
- Is in an environment that suits your personality, style and values
- Is supported by a management whose values are in alignment with yours
- Involves a business you believe in and support
- Operates within a structure that appreciates and recognizes your contributions
- Builds on and/or enhances your expertise and reputation in your field

See Introduction and chapter one for more details.

FIVE THINGS INTERVIEWERS SCRUTINIZE

1. Your skills and abilities: the things you actually do
2. Your personal characteristics and attitudes
3. Your ability to communicate
4. Your potential
5. How the interviewer feels about you

See chapter two for more details and examples.

WHAT TODAY'S EMPLOYERS EXPECT OF YOU

You will need to:

- Know yourself, your strengths and values
- Always look for new ways to contribute and take responsibility for your career path
- Cope with uncertainty and change
- Understand and appreciate diversity among people
- Be willing to try new approaches
- Be willing to wear several hats
- Know how to use computers
- Be service-oriented
- Appreciate the importance of and have good people skills
- Understand how the international marketplace can affect your particular business (it also helps to know other languages and cultures)
- Be self-motivated and confident
- Be willing to take risks
- Be dedicated to growing and seek continuing education
- Be willing to work on teams
- Have high standards and strive to be number one
- Have sound ethical judgment

See chapter two for more details.

FIVE THINGS THAT PUT YOU IN A POSITION OF STRENGTH

- Research: Find out what the company does, who runs it, their philosophy and culture, brief history and financial status.
- Know the pay range for the position and where you fit in.
- Coach and follow up with your references.
- Prepare answers and questions that reflect a "what can I do for you" attitude.
- Know your strengths, expertise, reason for job hunting and objective like the back of your hand.

See chapter two for more detail and specific examples.

FOUR-STEP EXERCISE TO EXPLAIN WHAT EVERY INTERVIEWER WANTS TO KNOW

Step 1: Know your strengths—the skills you enjoy using most and that come most naturally.

Step 2: Write out everything you know about—the body of knowledge you've acquired in your work and personal life and your experience.

Step 3: Develop a rationale for why you're job hunting—the facts only; not the emotional reasons or what it is you want to get away from.

Step 4: Create your objective—a statement that describes what you want to move toward and how you will contribute.

See chapter four for how to do this and examples.

HOW TO OVERCOME PRECONCEIVED NOTIONS AND HANDLE OBJECTIONS

1. Make a list of the qualities, experience and characteristics the ideal candidate would have.
2. Make a list of what the interviewer might be afraid you *won't* have.
3. Write down how the interviewer might define your "type." In other words, what are the preconceived notions the interviewer could have about you, based on your background?

Whether the interviewer subtly indicates his concern, comes out and says it or you just sense it, now you're ready to *deal with the objection* by:

1. Acknowledging the concern by either bringing it up or acknowledging it if it's mentioned.
2. Asking for more input: "Could you tell me more about your concern?"
3. Offering to clear up the concern or fill in with more information and giving an example that shows why the concern isn't an issue.

See chapter six for details on how to do this and examples.

SIX WAYS TO HOLD A POSITIVE, PRUDENT CONVERSATION WITH AN INTERVIEWER

- Avoid certain subjects, such as bosses, people problems and personal issues.
- Don't go in to the interview believing you're deficient or that the interviewer thinks you are.
- Be prepared for objections; acknowledge and resolve them.
- Don't talk too much.
- Don't go in with a hidden agenda to get back at a company or make someone look bad.
- Turn negatively stated questions around.

See chapter six for details and examples.

HOW TO SHOW YOUR POTENTIAL

Think of specific, concrete examples from your past work and personal life of how you used your strengths to solve problems or successfully complete a project. This is your proof that you will be valuable to the next employer. Write down each example by describing this information:

- What the problem was
- What you did to try to solve it
- What the result was

See chapter seven for details and examples.

HOW TO TALK ABOUT YOURSELF IN THREE MINUTES OR LESS

Interviewers are judging you by your communication skills. You need to develop a well-thought-out, brief, rehearsed—but not memorized word-for-word—presentation giving:

- A brief overview of where you've been, including your area of expertise, background and knowledge and why you're looking for a new position
- Your objective, including industries or areas you're exploring, what kind of position you're looking for, and—if this is a career change—a brief explanation on how your skills transfer and why you're interested in this field
- A few more details on you, including your strengths, positions you've held, an overview of your responsibilities and specific examples of how you've applied your strengths
- Your education if it's relevant and/or recent

After you've got a three-minute version, create a one-minute version. This will help you practice being concise, brief and relevant.

See chapter seven for details and loads of examples.

FIVE RULES OF ELEGANCE

1. Listen to the question. If you didn't hear or understand something, ask for clarification.
2. Only offer information that answers the question.
3. Think through and share relevant facts.
4. Take time to pause or reflect before you answer a question. A little silence is OK.
5. Only share positive information.

For more details and examples, see chapter seven.

YOUR GOALS IN THE SEVEN PHASES OF THE INTERVIEW

- Make a good first impression. You only get one chance.
- Listen for verbal and nonverbal clues that indicate if the interviewer likes or dislikes what she hears, is confused, supportive or wants more detail.
- Go with the flow. Don't try to take control.
- Take mental notes on what they're looking for, then let the interviewer know you've got it.
- Ask if you don't understand something.
- Weigh information to decide if the position is right.
- Always know where you stand. Ask: Do you think this is a good match?
- Always set up the next step. Ask: Where do we go from here?
- Set it up so *you* can check back.
- Check back to see where they are in the decision-making process.
- Don't make hasty judgments, but do pay attention to clues on how you're treated and what their priorities seem to be.
- Always present yourself in the best possible light.

See chapter eight for details.

TYPES OF QUESTIONS AND WHY INTERVIEWERS ASK THEM

1. *Questions about your skills and work experience.* They want to know what you can do and where you have done it, why you want to do it, why you want to do it here, why you're qualified, what you'll do for them, how you handle situations.
2. *Questions about your knowledge.* They want to know what you know, how you'll make a difference with that, how you've made a difference in the past, how you will stay current.
3. *Questions about your personal characteristics.* They want to know what kind of person you are, how you handle situations and your overall style and priorities.

See chapter nine for suggested phrases to use, what not to share and guidelines in giving appropriate answers to common and not-so-common interview questions.

NINE RULES FOR ANSWERING INTERVIEW QUESTIONS

- Know your skills and work experience, how and why you've been successful and have stories to prove it.
- Share the facts, then stop talking.
- Know "what you know" (your knowledge and expertise), how you learned it, how you stay current, how you'll make a difference and have stories to prove it.
- Know what kind of person you are and how you handle things, situations and people and have stories to prove it.
- Stick to information that demonstrates you have the skills, experience and education to do the job.
- Know what questions are appropriate and inappropriate for employers to ask.
- If you hear inappropriate questions, ask what the question has to do with the job.
- Always take the high road.
- As good as you think you are, plan your answers and practice, practice, practice.

See chapter nine for details and examples.

THREE THINGS TO DO BEFORE YOU NEGOTIATE A JOB OFFER

- Promise yourself: I will not discuss salary until I'm offered the position.
- Know two figures: 1. What you'd love to make, and 2. What you'll settle for.
- Learn and practice key phrases to deal with the interviewer's probing about what salary you're making (or were making) and want to make in your next job.

See chapter ten for details and examples.

COMMON INTERVIEW MISTAKES AND HOW TO OVERCOME THEM

Mistake #1. You feel pressured to have all the right answers and do all the right things to get the job.

Solution: It's not as tough as you're making it. The interview isn't a performance where you have to deliver your lines with perfection and persuade your audience to buy you. It's an opportunity to present yourself in the best possible light while you explore if the job is a good fit. Just go in and have a conversation—on your best behavior. See Introduction for more detail.

Mistake #2: You believe employers are trying to trick you by the questions they ask. If you believe this, it can show in your attitude. You may figure, "Why bother preparing, they're just trying to trip me up." So you go in unprepared and then blame "them" for your poor performance.

Solution: Sorry, folks, but most questions are pretty logical and help interviewers decide if you're a good fit for the job and the company. They aren't tricky if you put yourself in interviewers' shoes and understand why they're asking. See chapters five and nine for details.

Mistake #3: You have a "what can you do for me" attitude. That's where you go into the interview thinking: I have to solve *my* problem, which is to find a job . . . how much they'll pay me and what kind of benefits and vacation I get.

Solution: Put your troubles behind you. Companies don't hire you to give you a job, money, benefits and vacation. They hire you because you have the skills to solve their problems. Turn your thinking around to: "What can I do for you? What are your problems? OK, now let me tell you how I can solve them to make your business better and more profitable." See chapter two for more detail.

Mistake #4: You wing the interview. No wonder you're not getting any offers. Poor communication skills alone is reason to eliminate you. If you give half-baked answers and haven't prepared for the most common interview questions, you're not going to be a very effective communicator.

Solution: See the interview as an important give-and-take conversation where your words must be carefully chosen, well thought out, and must address the concerns or issues on the interviewer's mind. Read chapter nine and prepare for these questions. Write out your answers. Practice them. Record yourself.

Mistake #5: You talk too much. You give unsolicited information, talk about your troubles, your anger, your annoying boss or your crummy job, or bore the interviewer to tears with endless details.

Solution: Listen to the question, think through what you need to share to answer the question, then zip your lip. This is not the place to air dirty laundry, tell your life story since elementary school, or to tell the truth, the whole truth and nothing but the truth. It's an opportunity to share honest, relevant, pertinent, positive, concise information that shows the interviewer how skilled you are, what a terrific person you are and how you can contribute to the organization. See chapter six for more detail.

Mistake #6: You talk about salary too soon. "Too" soon means anytime before you know the company thinks you're the hottest thing since sliced bread. You'll know that when the interviewer makes you an offer.

Solution: Don't ask about salary and benefits. If interviewers bring it up, let them know that it's not your first priority. Keep the conversation on the job, not the pay. See chapter ten for more detail.

Mistake #7: You're late for the interview. This says the world about you: You don't care enough to get there on time, you don't respect other people's schedules and time, details are not important and you will treat your job the same way.

Solution: Don't be late for this very important date. Set two alarm clocks, fill your gas tank the night before, drive to the company beforehand so you know where it is and give yourself extra time to get there. See chapter eight.

Mistake #8: You didn't do your homework. You go into an interview and you don't really understand what the company does, who runs it, its history, its goals and the issues it faces in the industry.

You can't answer the most common questions, such as: Why do you want to work here? What can you do for our company? What do you know about us?

Solution: Make it your business to thoroughly research the company. Go to the library, go online and talk to people who know the company. Make research a given, not an optional task that you think about the night before the interview. See chapter four.

Mistake #9: You don't participate in the conversation. For whatever reason—because you don't know what to ask or you're shy—you don't ask questions. This gets interpreted as disinterest.

Solution: Get comfortable asking questions. Know what you want to say when you go into interviews so you'll feel more confident. Develop a list of five questions you can ask or points to discuss. Practice asking questions on a tape recorder. See yourself as a confident communicator who has something worthwhile to say. See chapter four.

Mistake #10: You give away your control. You do this when you call someone to follow up on a letter, a meeting or just to touch base, they're out of the office or on the phone, and you leave a message for them to call you back. (Odds are this will happen at least half the time you try to call someone.)

Solution: Unless it's your mother or spouse, your job search is not a priority with most other people. Your job search is *your* job. So when the secretary says, "He's not in . . . give me your number and I'll have him call you back," tell the secretary you'll be in and out a lot, and ask when a good time to call the person back is. See chapter eight.

Mistake #11: The "What Ifs" take over. These are those fears that plague you when things aren't going the way you want. You've had an interview, you haven't heard back and begin "what iffing": "What if they really didn't like me . . . they found out what I was making at my last job and think they can't afford me . . . my old boss said something bad about me . . . that comment I made about not wanting to work weekends ruined everything. . . ." This type of thinking makes you paranoid and gets you concentrating on the wrong issues.

Solution: Accept that you can't change the past or control how someone else thinks or acts. Then quit worrying. Get clarification on what the other party is thinking. And don't leave interviews without some idea of the next step. Set up a date to talk again or an arrangement that if you haven't heard back by a specific date, it's OK for you to call. See chapter eight.

INDEX

More Great Books to Help You Get the Most Out of Life!

Cover Letters That Will Get You the Job You Want—Discover how to introduce yourself and your resume compellingly and efficiently with a well-written, well-constructed cover letter. Includes 100 tested cover letters that work! *#70185/$12.99/192 pages/paperback*

The Selling-From-Home Sourcebook—Work from home, meet people and make money at the same time! With this unique reference, you'll learn to define your goals as you explore a wealth of advice on setting up your own home-based sales business. You'll also discover a world of information about careers in sales, plus listings of over 100 companies that offer home-based selling opportunities.
#70316/$17.99/224 pages/paperback

The Edge Resume & Job Search Strategy—Job Hunters—learn to create the kind of resumes that will stand out in a stack—and use them to open the right doors. *#70298/$23.95/172 pages/paperback*

How to Have a 48-Hour Day—Get more done and have more fun as you double what you can do in a day! Aslett reveals reasons to be more productive everywhere—and what "production" actually is. You'll learn how to keep accomplishing despite setbacks, ways to boost effectiveness, the things that help your productivity and much more. *#70339/$12.99/160 pages/120 illus./paperback*

Stephanie Culp's 12-Month Organizer and Project Planner—This is the get it done planner! If you have projects you're burning to start or yearning to finish, you'll zoom toward accomplishment by using these forms, "To-Do" lists, checklists and calendars. *#70274/$12.99/192 pages/paperback*

How to Run a Family Business—To ensure your family business stays afloat, you need sound advice. You'll find everything you need to know, from forming a board of directors, to setting salaries in this indispensable resource. *#70214/$14.95/176 pages/paperback*

The Complete Guide to Building and Outfitting an Office in Your Home—You'll discover how to convert basements and attics, determine space needs, create layouts—even specifics like how to keep house sounds out! *#70244/$18.99/176 pages/105 b&w illus./paperback*

Friends & Lovers: How to Meet the People You Want to Meet—Discover how to turn your favorite activities into a personal action plan for meeting people! *#01294/$12.99/202 pages/paperback*

Cleaning Up for a Living—Learn from the best! Don Aslett shares with you the tricks and tips he used to build a $12 million commercial cleaning business. *#70016/$16.99/208 pages/paperback*

Single Person's Guide to Buying A Home—This buying guide offers you worksheets and checklists that show you what to look for when buying a home on your own.
#70200/$14.95/144 pages/paperback

How to Start Making Money with Your Crafts—Launch a rewarding crafts business with this guide that starts with the basics—from creating marketable products to setting the right prices—and explores all the exciting possibilities. End-of-chapter quizzes, worksheets, ideas and lessons learned by successful crafters are included to increase your learning curve. *#70302/$18.99/176 pages/35 b&w illus.*

Speaking With Confidence: A Guidebook for Public Speakers—Tips and exercises show you how to overcome stage fright and improve your speaking abilities. *#70101/$9.95/176 pages/paperback*

How To Get Organized When You Don't Have the Time—You keep meaning to organize the closet and clean out the garage, but who has the time? Culp combines proven time-management principles with practical ideas to help you clean-up key trouble spots in a hurry. *#01354/$11.99/216 pages/paperback*

Homemade Money, 5th Edition—With the all-new edition of this comprehensive guide, you'll be up to speed on the legal matters, accounting practices, tax laws and marketing techniques sure to make your home-based business a success! *#70231/$19.99/400 pages/paperback*

Don Aslett's Clutter-Free! Finally and Forever—Free yourself of unnecessary stuff that chokes your home and clogs your life! If you feel owned by your belongings, you'll discover incredible excuses people use for allowing clutter, how to beat the "no-time" excuse, how to determine what's junk, how to prevent recluttering and much more! *#70306/$12.99/224 pages/50 illus./paperback*

The Inventor's Handbook: How to Develop, Protect, & Market Your Invention, 2nd Edition—Provides practicing and prospective inventors with the tools to take their ideas from concept to production to marketing. *#70062/$14.95/232 pages/paperback*

Mortgage Loans: What's Right for You?—Don't make a big-money mistake signing for the wrong mortgage! Find the facts on the types of mortgages perfectly suited to your needs and financial situation. Plus, get information on caps, margins, points and more! *#70242/$14.99/144 pages/paperback*

Export-Import—Get the vocabulary, insider tips and rules of the game you need to compete in rapidly expanding world markets. This revised edition will help you stay on top of the competition with the latest information on trade laws and government regulations including those for NAFTA and GATT. *#70285/$16.99/160 pages/paperback*